EDWARD FITZGERALD

BY

A. C. BENSON

FELLOW OF MAGDALENE COLLEGE, CAMBRIDGE

LONDON: MACMILLAN & CO., LIMITED

NINETEEN HUNDRED AND FIVE

Republished, 1970
Scholarly Press, 22929 Industrial Drive East
St. Clair Shores, Michigan 48080

Library of Congress Catalog Card Number:71-131625
Standard Book Number 403-00512-4

This edition is printed on a high-quality,
acid-free paper that meets specification
requirements for fine book paper referred
to as "300-year" paper

ENGLISH MEN OF LETTERS

EDWARD FITZGERALD

CONTENTS

PREFATORY NOTE

THE principal books which I have consulted, and to which reference is made in the following pages, besides FitzGerald's own publications, are the following:—

Letters and Literary Remains of Edward FitzGerald, 3 vols. (Macmillan & Co.), 1889; *Letters of Edward FitzGerald*, 2 vols. (Macmillan & Co.), 1901; *Letters of Edward FitzGerald to Fanny Kemble* (1871-1883), (Richard Bentley & Son), 1895; *More Letters of Edward FitzGerald* (Macmillan & Co.), 1901; *Miscellanies*, by Edward FitzGerald (Macmillan & Co.), 1900—the above all edited by Mr. William Aldis Wright.

The Life of Edward FitzGerald, 2 vols., by Thomas Wright (Grant Richards), 1904; *The Life of Edward FitzGerald*, by John Glyde (introduction by Edward Clodd), (C. Arthur Pearson), 1900; *Two Suffolk Friends*, by Francis Hindes Groome (Blackwood), 1895; *Life and Letters of Edward Byles Cowell*, by George Cowell (Macmillan), 1904.

In studying the *Omar Khayyám* by FitzGerald, I have found specially useful the volume containing the four editions published in the poet's lifetime (Macmillan), 1902; the volume entitled *Edward FitzGerald's Rubá'iyát of Omar Khayyám, with their original Persian Sources collated from his own MSS., and literally translated*,

by Edward Heron-Allen (Bernard Quaritch), 1899; a
volume containing the *Rubá'iyát*, with a commentary
by H. M. Batson, and an introduction by Principal
E. D. Ross (Methuen), 1900; and for general purposes,
A Literary History of Persia, by Professor E. G. Browne
(Fisher Unwin), 1902.

For the Bibliography I have been enabled to consult
the *Chronological List* of Edward FitzGerald's books,
printed by the Caxton Club, Chicago, 1899, and the
Notes for a Bibliography of Edward FitzGerald, reprinted
from *Notes and Queries*, 1900.

I have also consulted the *Dictionary of National Biography*, together with other critical and biographical
essays and articles.

I take this opportunity of thanking the following
for help, advice, and criticism.   Mr. W. Aldis Wright,
who has very kindly and readily answered my questions, and lent me interesting unpublished documents;
Mr. James Fitzmaurice-Kelly, who has given me simply
invaluable assistance in the section dealing with Fitz-
Gerald's translations from Calderon; Mr. Thomas
Wright, for kind permission to make use of his *Life
of Edward FitzGerald*, which is a mine of detailed
information about the poet's daily life and movements;
Mr. John Glyde, for a similar permission; Mr. Edward
Heron-Allen, for permission to quote from his transla-
tion mentioned above; Mr. Edmund Gosse, Mr. Percy
Lubbock, Mr. Howard O. Sturgis, and other friends.

A. C. B.

EDWARD FITZGERALD

CHAPTER I

EARLY YEARS

THE life that it is here proposed to depict was a life singularly devoid of incident. It was the career of a lonely, secluded, fastidious, and affectionate man; it was a life not rich in results, not fruitful in example. It is the history of a few great friendships, much quiet benevolence, tender loyalty, wistful enjoyment. The tangible results are a single small volume of imperishable quality, some accomplished translations of no great literary importance, a little piece of delicate prose-writing, and many beautiful letters.

But over the whole is the indefinable charm of temperament and personality. The background is so minute, so uneventful, that it is only possible to draw a Dutch picture, so to speak, of the scene, not slurring over details, nor discarding homely touches, but depicting with careful fidelity the trivial round of little incidents and pleasures in which FitzGerald was more or less content to live.

It may be thought that there is an excess of extracts from the letters; but FitzGerald had a marvellous power of dipping and steeping the minute circumstances of his life in the subtle and evasive personality which is the essence of the man. He

A

contrived to cast, by a style of wonderful purity and individuality, a delicate aroma of reflection, of pathos, of charm, over facts and thoughts that have but little distinct and actual significance. And therefore I have endeavoured to let FitzGerald speak much for himself, because I believe that it is the only true method of giving an impression of a character that, in spite of eccentricity, listlessness, and melancholy, possessed a rich and subtle attractiveness that is sometimes denied to figures of more vital force and more supreme achievement.

Edward FitzGerald was born on the 31st of March 1809. It is a fascinating but somewhat delusive task to try to trace the origins of genius. A great writer is often the outcome of a vigorous stock which has done nothing to exhaust its artistic vitality, but has slowly matured among simple pursuits; as for immediate precursors, a mother of strong feeling and a father of mild literary tastes would seem to afford the best possibilities; but, as a matter of fact, it would be difficult to devise a *milieu* more incongruous with the temperament and preoccupations of Edward FitzGerald than that in which he was actually born.

His father and mother were first cousins; his father was John Purcell, son of a wealthy Irish doctor, a Dublin man, who traced his descent from Cromwell; among the family relics were the Protector's sword and watch. FitzGerald's mother was Mary Frances FitzGerald, herself the child of first cousins, and descended from the Earls of Kildare. His maternal grandfather was a man of great wealth, with estates in Ireland, Northamptonshire, Suffolk, and elsewhere. Upon his death in 1818, John Purcell, FitzGerald's father, assumed his wife's surname, she being her

father's heiress. "I somehow detest my own scrol-
loping surname," wrote our hero at the end of his life
to Mr. Aldis Wright.

Edward FitzGerald was the seventh of eight children.
His father was a typical country squire, fond of hunting
and shooting, and M.P. for Seaford; but had an unbalanced vein in him, a tendency to nurse unpractical
schemes, which eventually led to financial disaster;
FitzGerald's mother was a vivid, gifted woman, of
fashionable and social tastes, a good linguist, and fond
of poetry. Her portrait by Sir Thomas Lawrence, to
whom she more than once sat, shows a face of a
haughty type, with bold dark eyes, an aquiline nose,
black lustrous hair, and a small thin-lipped mouth,
which gives an imperious and not wholly agreeable
look to the face. Her children admired her intensely,
but felt rather awe than love for the majestic and
superb lady. The FitzGeralds lived in considerable
splendour. The house in which Edward was born
was the White House, Bredfield (now called Bredfield
House), a stately, plastered, Jacobean mansion near
Woodbridge. They had a town-house in Portland
Place, as well as a Manor-house at Naseby, called
Naseby Woolleys, where some of FitzGerald's early
life was spent. There was another house on an
estate at Seaford, and another at Castle Irwell, near
Manchester. They owned pictures, old china, and
gold plate; they had a box at the Haymarket;
Mrs. FitzGerald drove about in a coach-and-four.
Mr. FitzGerald spent money profusely on his stable,
his electioneering expenses, his shooting. He seems
to have had little head for business; he was robbed
by his bailiffs; but his fortune could have stood
considerable inroads had he not conceived a wild
design of digging for coal under his Manchester pro-

perty, a scheme which was eventually to engulph a great part of his fortune.

When Edward was five years old, his father took a house in Paris; and several months were spent there in each of the next few years. In 1821 the boy went to King Edward's School, Bury St. Edmunds, under Dr. Malkin. He retained a pleasant recollection of this portly, genial, handsome, energetic man, whose lameness did not detract from his dignity; and of the vivacity and kindness of Mrs. Malkin. The school had a great reputation, and Dr. Malkin paid special attention to the writing of English. From his school-days date several of FitzGerald's lifelong friendships. Among his boy-friends were William Bodham Donne (1807-1882), the well-known historical writer, and eventually Licenser of Plays; J. M. Kemble (1807-1857), the famous Anglo-Saxon scholar; and James Spedding (1808-1881), the editor of Bacon, a man of real though secluded genius.

In 1825 the FitzGeralds left Bredfield and moved to a fine house near Ipswich, Wherstead Lodge, which had previously been let to Lord Granville, with the shooting, for £1000 a year; it was famous for its collection of pictures, and contained works by Hogarth, Cosway, Kneller, Lely, and Reynolds.

Up to this time there is little in the records which would enable one to forecast the boy's future fame. He was fond of books, fond of the country and the sea; and with a great devotion to the theatre. The home life had been happy and full of stir; he had more experience of the world than most boys of his age; there was a good deal of wilfulness in the family, and independence of temperament, which developed later into strong eccentricity in more than one member of the circle. Two traits of character, however, can be

traced from an early age; one was FitzGerald's gift
for idealising his friends, which led in after-life to
some very true and sacred friendships, and also to
some inconvenient sentimentality : the other was the
boy's perception of and delight in individualities and
oddities of character. The neighbourhood of Woodbridge seems to have been rich in singular specimens
of humanity. Such was Squire Jenny, a near neighbour, a jovial, vigorous old sportsman, of short stature
and with enormous ears, who lived with open windows,
in carpetless rooms, into which the snow was allowed
to drift; his house presided over by a miserly sister,
who hoarded money like a magpie, and practised a
sordid frugality. Another such was a portly old
Anglo-Indian, Major Moor, who wore a huge white
hat, many sizes too big for him, and carried a stick
made from the timbers of the *Royal George*. The
Major collected images of Oriental gods, which he
eventually immured in a pyramidal mausoleum near his
front drive. He was always ready to walk with the
boy, and would talk for the hour together about the
racy provincialisms of the countryside, and about his
Eastern experiences. To this influence we can con-
fidently trace FitzGerald's early taste for expressive
local words, and his interest in Oriental literature.
Indeed Major Moor can, perhaps, be dignified with the
title of the true begetter of the Omar Khayyám.

The boy's delight in these singular persons, his
appreciation of their personalities, their ways, their
idiosyncrasies, show that his perception, his interest,
and his observation were even at this early age both
keen and humorous.

Edward FitzGerald was one who lived all his life
with a wistful and tender outlook upon the past. The
old stories, the old days, had always a kind of gentle

consecration for him; one of the latest visits he ever
paid was to see the old school at Bury; and there is
a little reminiscence of him, when quite an old man,
in one of the half-whimsical, half-tender moods which
characterised him, going through the grounds of Bredfield, and refusing to enter the house; but gazing
curiously in at the windows of the so-called "Magistrate's Room," because it was there that he used to
be whipped.

In October 1826, at the age of seventeen, Fitz-
Gerald went into residence at Cambridge, entering
Trinity College; he lodged with a Mrs. Perry, at
No. 19, King's Parade, the house having been since
rebuilt. The windows looked out on the fantastic
screen of King's College, then just completed, the
gate-house crowned with heavy pinnacles, and the
austere and towering east front of the College Chapel.
The Master of Trinity was Christopher Wordsworth,
a younger brother of the poet, a man of majestic
appearance and donnish manners. He was named by
FitzGerald and his irreverent friends "the Meeserable
Sinner," from his affected manner of responding in the
College Chapel; and the epithet was transferred to
"Daddy" Wordsworth—as FitzGerald loved to call the
bard—whom they named the "Meeserable Poet." Chief
among FitzGerald's friends was W. M. Thackeray,
then settled in rooms on the ground-floor of the great
court of Trinity, near the chapel. The other members
of the circle were John Allen, afterwards Archdeacon
of Salop, a guileless, vigorous, and straightforward
youth, of whom Bishop Lonsdale long afterwards wrote
that he had never met a man who feared God more,
or man less; W. H. Thompson, afterwards the famous
Master of Trinity; Frank Edgeworth, the brother of
the authoress; Robert Groome, afterwards Archdeacon

of Suffolk ; Charles Buller—then fresh from the tute-
lage of Carlyle—who was to die prematurely before
he attained the parliamentary fame which seemed
surely awaiting him ; Frederick Maurice, the theological
philosopher ; John M. Kemble ; Blakesley, afterwards
Dean of Lincoln ; Merivale, the historian, afterwards
Dean of Ely ; James Spedding ; and Richard Monckton-
Milnes, afterwards Lord Houghton. Richard Trench,
afterwards Archbishop of Dublin, and the Tennysons,
Frederic,[1] Charles, and Alfred, were FitzGerald's contemporaries at Cambridge, but he did not come to
know them until a later date.

It is a remarkable group of men ; and perhaps the
most notable fact is that though many of them
drifted apart from each other, yet FitzGerald, recluse
as he was, continued to keep up affectionate relations
with nearly all of them throughout life. "What
passions our friendships were !" wrote Thackeray of
those undergraduate days.   Friendships remained
passions for FitzGerald.

As might have been expected, FitzGerald was not
an earnest student. He pottered about, read such
classical authors as he liked in a desultory way ;
occupied himself with water-colour drawing, music,
and poetry. He cared nothing for the political and

---

[1] Frederic Tennyson, elder brother of Alfred, was born in
1807 ; he took his degree in 1832. He married in 1839 Maria
Giuliotti, daughter of the chief magistrate of Siena, and took
up his abode in Florence, where he lived for twenty years,
afterwards moving to Jersey. He had a certain lyrical gift, but
was overshadowed by his brother's fame, and his poems, *Days
and Hours*, published in 1854, had little success. Between
1890 and 1895 he published three volumes of verse ; he was at
one time much under the dominion of mystical and Swedenborgian ideas ; many of FitzGerald's best letters were written
to him, though after early life they never met.

social aspirations which set his companions aglow;
he walked, talked, strolled into his friends' rooms;
he smoked, drank coffee, sang songs, and exchanged
sketches with Thackeray. He had plenty of money,
but no expensive tastes. His wardrobe was in a
perpetual condition of dilapidation, insomuch that
when his majestic mother rattled into Cambridge,
with her yellow coach and four black horses, like
a fairy queen, and sent a man-servant to acquaint
FitzGerald with her arrival, he had no boots in
which to attend her summons.

There are two little pencil sketches of FitzGerald
as an undergraduate, drawn possibly by Spedding, now
in the possession of Mr. Aldis Wright, of great interest.
In these he appears as a tall, loosely built youth, care-
lessly dressed, with rather full and prominent lips, of an
ingenuous and pleasing aspect; in one, a three-quarter
face, he wears a smiling air. In the other, there is a
pathetic droop of the brows which gives the face a
sadder expression, more like his later look.

In these days FitzGerald nursed far-reaching literary
projects, and was by no means devoid of ambitious
dreams. He wrote long afterwards to Frederic Tennyson :—

"I have been . . . to visit a parson in Dorsetshire. He
wore cap and gown when I did at Cambridge—together did
we roam the fields about Grantchester, discuss all things,
thought ourselves fine fellows, and that one day we should
make a noise in the world. He is now a poor Rector in one
of the most out-of-the-way villages in England—has five children—fats and kills his pig—smokes his pipe—loves his home
and cares not ever to be seen or heard of out of it. I was
amused with his company ; he much pleased to see me : we
had not met face to face for fifteen years ; and now both of
us such very sedate, unambitious people !"

The whole Cambridge life was a delightful one, and

exactly suited FitzGerald's temperament. He contrived to take a degree in 1830; and then began a
vague, drifting, leisurely existence which ended only
with his death. He had money enough for his wants;
there was no need for him to adopt a profession, and
it appears that no pressure was put upon him to induce
him to do so. Probably a man with FitzGerald's disposition both gained and lost by the absence of definite
occupation. He often lamented it himself, but he was
too irresolute to embrace a discipline which might have,
so to speak, pulled him together. Perhaps if he had
been forced to work for a livelihood, he would have
been more careful of time; perhaps steady work would
have cleared off the vapours, and left him more desirous
to use his hours of leisure. It is practically certain
that one in whom the instinct for literary work was
so definite as it was in FitzGerald, would somehow
or other have contrived to write. But, on the other
hand, definite occupation would have affected the
quality of FitzGerald's writing. It is hardly conceiv-
able that he could have been successful in the capacity
of a professional man, though his patience and his love
of finish might have made him a competent official;
if his life had been thus ordered, we might have
had more translations of Greek and Spanish plays,
and more literary essays; but we should hardly have
had Omar; and certainly not the incomparable letters.

So FitzGerald floated out upon the world; he went
for a long visit to a married sister, Mrs. Kerrich, who
lived at a pleasant place, Geldestone Hall, near
Beccles. After this he was to be found at Paris staying with an aunt, and in the company of Thackeray,
who professed to be studying art. But it seems
that Thackeray's visit to Paris was a clandestine
one, kept secret from his parents; he had even told
his college tutor that he was to spend his vacation

in Huntingdonshire.   Thackeray enjoyed himself at
the time, but repented at leisure.   He said afterwards that he never crossed the Channel without
thinking regretfully of the episode : "Guilt, sir, guilt
remains stamped on the memory."   From an endless
round of gaieties, breakfasts, evening parties, theatres,
FitzGerald escaped with a firm resolve to become "a
great bear."   He reached Southampton, where he fell
in with Allen, who, in the course of a walk to Netley,
"tried to make him steady in his views on religion."

After this FitzGerald went off to the paternal estate
of Naseby, where he lodged at a farmhouse ; and here
he settled down to the kind of life that he thoroughly
enjoyed : books, walks, and the company of simple
village people, dining with the village carpenter, and
going to church "quite the king" in a brave, blue
frock-coat.

Here it was that he wrote that beautiful lyric,
"The Meadows in Spring," which has so sweet an
intermingled flavour of old and new.

> " 'Tis a dull sight
>   To see the year dying,
> When winter winds
>   Set the yellow wood sighing :
>   Sighing, oh ! sighing.
>
> When such a time cometh,
>   I do retire
> Into an old room
>   Beside a bright fire :
>   Oh, pile a bright fire !
>
> And there I sit
>   Reading old things,
> Of knights and lorn damsels
>   While the wind sings—
>   Oh, drearily sings !

I never look out
  Nor attend to the blast ;
For all to be seen
  Is the leaves falling fast :
    Falling, falling !

But close at the hearth,
  Like a cricket, sit I,
Reading of summer
  And chivalry—
    Gallant chivalry !

Then with an old friend
  I talk of our youth—
How 'twas gladsome, but often
  Foolish, forsooth :
    But gladsome, gladsome !

Or to get merry
  We sing some old rhyme,
That made the wood ring again
  In summer time—
    Sweet summer time !

Then go we to smoking,
  Silent and snug :
Nought passes between us,
  Save a brown jug—
    Sometimes !

And sometimes a tear
  Will rise in each eye,
Seeing the two old friends
  So merrily—
    So merrily !

And ere to bed [1]
  Go we, go we,

---

[1] There is another version of the tenth stanza, in a probably earlier book :—

    " So winter passeth
      Like a long sleep
    From falling autumn
      To primrose-peep."

Down on the ashes
    We kneel on the knee,
        Praying together !

Thus, then, live I,
    Till, 'mid all the gloom,
By Heaven ! the bold sun
    Is with me in the room
        Shining, shining !

Then the clouds part,
    Swallows soaring between ;
The spring is alive,
    And the meadows are green !

I jump up, like mad,
    Break the old pipe in twain,
And away to the meadows,
    The meadows again !"

It is difficult to praise this charming lyric too highly ;
but two points are especially noteworthy in it : firstly,
that a young man of twenty-two should have written
a poem which is all touched with a sense of wistful
retrospect, is very characteristic of the author ; and
secondly, from the technical point of view, we may
note the real literary skill shown in the construction
of the stanzas ; the unrhymed fifth line, which ends
all but the last two stanzas, acts as a delicate refrain
or echo ; and, in particular, the last line of the sixth
stanza, "But gladsome, gladsome," follows with the
subtlest charm the pause of reflective thought.

The poem appeared in Hone's *Year-Book* in 1831, and
again in the *Athenæum*, slightly altered, on July 9 of the
same year. It was by some supposed to be the work of
Charles Lamb ; and that Charles Lamb would willingly
have been the author is proved by his writing of it :
"The *Athenæum* has been hoaxed with some exquisite
poetry." . . . "'Tis a poem that I envy—that and

Montgomery's 'Last Man'—I envy the writers because
I feel I could have done something like them."

To this period also belong the brisk lines "To Will
Thackeray":

> " The chair that Will sat in I sit in the best,
>   The tobacco is sweetest which Willy has blest " ;

and the following year, 1832, the beautiful lines "To
a Lady singing":

> " Canst thou, my Clora, declare,
>   After thy sweet song dieth
>   Into the wild summer air,
>   Whither it falleth or flieth ?
>   Soon would my answer be noted ·
>   Wert thou but sage as sweet-throated.
>
>   Melody, dying away,
>   Into the dark sky closes,
>   Like the good soul from her clay
>   Like the fair odour of roses ;
>   Therefore thou now art behind it,
>   But thou shalt follow, and find it."

Two stanzas were afterwards added, but without
improving the song:

> " Nothing can utterly die :
>   Music aloft up-springing
>   Turns to pure atoms of sky
>   Each golden note of thy singing :
>   And that to which morning did listen
>   At eve in a rainbow may glisten.
>
>   Beauty when laid in the grave
>   Feedeth the lily beside her,
>   Therefore her soul cannot have
>   Station or honour denied her ;
>   She will not better her essence,
>   But wear a crown in God's presence."

FitzGerald was reading at the time Hazlitt's *Poets*,

and his letters are full of allusions to old English
lyrists—such writers as Carew, Wotton, Donne, and
Fletcher. But the wonder is that a man who at such
an age could write such original, mature, and well-
proportioned lyrics, should not have cared to pursue
the quest. His other scattered lyrics, which it is as
well to summarise here, are a little "Elegy to Anne
Allen," sister of his friend, who died in 1830; "The
Old Beau" and "The Merchant's Daughter" (1834),
the former of which is a pretty poem of the school of
Praed; "Bredfield Hall" (1839), which he himself
rated highly, but which is nothing more than a
languid Tennysonian lyric, with several metrical
lapses, "Chronomoros" (probably about 1840), a
somewhat jingling melody, with a philosophical
motive; a tiny idyll, "Virgil's Garden," a paraphrase
of the passage from the Fourth *Georgic* about the
Corycian old man, a sonnet translated from Petrarch,
a verse "To a Violet," and some wretched memorial
lines to Bernard Barton (1849).

We get glimpses of FitzGerald in these early years
wandering like the Scholar-Gipsy. Now he is in
London buying books; now he is staying at Tenby with
the Allens. From this last visit dates one of the most
romantic friendships of FitzGerald's life. This new
friend was a young fellow, William Kenworthy Browne
by name, son of a Bedford alderman. He was fond
of amusement, a keen rider, a good shot, a fisherman,
a billiard player, but with an affectionate disposition,
and a great fund of sterling common-sense; moreover,
not averse to books and literature, when pleasantly
interpreted. FitzGerald, writing more than twenty-
three years after to Mrs. Allen, said :—

"I owe to Tenby the chance acquaintance of another Person
who now from that hour remains one of my very best Friends.

A Lad—then just 16—whom I met on board the Packet
from Bristol : and next morning at the Boarding House—apt
then to appear with a little *chalk* on the edge of his Cheek
from a touch of the Billiard Table Cue—and now a man of 40
—Farmer, Magistrate, Militia Officer—Father of a Family—
of more use in a week than I in my Life long. You too have
six sons, your Letter tells me. They may do worse than do
as well as he I have spoken of, though he too has sown some
wild oats, and paid for doing so."

He went in 1834 to stay with the Brownes at
Cauldwell House in Cauldwell Street, Bedford, and
hardly a year passed until Browne's marriage without one or more of these visits. It well illustrates
FitzGerald's power of inspiring and maintaining a
friendship, that so close a tie should have existed
between two natures that would not have appeared at
first sight congenial ; and it also illustrates FitzGerald's
marvellous power of taking people as he found them,
and loving them for what they were, with no desire to
mould them to his own will.

Another of FitzGerald's chief friends and associates
in early years was Bernard Barton, a Quaker, who had
been for a short time in business in Woodbridge, but in
1808 became a clerk in Messrs. Alexander's bank there.
He was a most industrious composer of verse, only
remarkable for its firm grasp of the obvious, which yet
from its homely sentiment and domestic piety attained
a certain vogue, and gave Barton a temporary position
in the literary world. Barton was, moreover, a great
letter-writer, and corresponded regularly with several
eminent authors. Some of Charles Lamb's most
delightful letters are written to him. Bernard Barton's health was at one time considerably affected by
his sedentary life ; after working in the bank all day,
he would spend the evening writing verse, and sit up

to a late hour finishing a poem. His letters to his friends are full of complaints of headache and low spirits. Southey gave him excellent advice in return, recommending him to go early to bed and avoid suppers. Charles Lamb, in his most characteristic vein, blended advice with fantastic rhetoric:—

"You are much too apprehensive," he wrote, "about your complaint. I know many that are always ailing of it, and live on to a good old age. . . . Believe the general sense of the mercantile world, which holds that desks are not deadly. It is the mind, good B. B., and not the limbs, that faints by long sitting. Think of the patience of tailors—think how long the Lord Chancellor sits—think of the brooding hen."

At another time Bernard Barton announced his intention of giving up his post and earning a livelihood by writing. Charles Lamb replied in a charming letter expressing the utmost horror at the idea:— "Keep to your bank, and the bank will keep you. . . . O the corroding, torturing, tormenting thoughts that disturb the brain of the unlucky wight, who must draw upon it for daily sustenance! Henceforth I retract all my fond complaints of mercantile employment; look upon them as lovers' quarrels. I was but half in earnest. Welcome dead timber of a desk, that makes me live!"

Bernard Barton's position was, however, made easier by a gift of £1200 from some wealthy Quakers and relations of his own; and in 1845 Sir Robert Peel, after asking him to dinner in Whitehall, procured for him a Civil List pension of £100 a year. Barton wrote far too much and corrected far too little to attain to any permanent position in poetry. FitzGerald, who wrote a brief memoir of Barton after his death, said that there was a kind of youthful impetuosity about

him which could not be restrained. He was as eager
for every one else to write verse as he was to write it
himself ; he had no envy, and would scarcely admit a
fault in the verses of others, whether private friends or
public authors. Barton lived a simple life with his
only daughter, devoted to literature of a higher kind ;
FitzGerald was a constant visitor at the house ; and
there must have been a great charm about the old
Quaker, the charm of unembarrassed simplicity. His
gentle egotism, his unaffected enthusiasm made him a
welcome visitor alike at Whitehall and in a country
cottage.

FitzGerald, who was alive to his weaknesses, describes
him as "a very strange character ; a good-natured and
benevolent person, with a good deal of pride and
caution, with a pretence at humility ; perverse, formal,
strict, plain, and unpresuming in his dress—a great
many contradictions of character," and again he spoke
of Barton as "looking very demurely to the necessary
end of life."

In 1835 FitzGerald paid a memorable visit to the
home of his friend, James Spedding, at Mirehouse,
near Bassenthwaite Lake, under Skiddaw, Tennyson
being his fellow-guest.

The friends rambled about, talked, smoked and read.
Late at night in the silent house Tennyson would
declaim, in a voice like the murmur of a pinewood,
out of a little red book, some of the poems afterwards
to become immortal. Spedding was not allowed to
read aloud, because Tennyson said that he read too
much as if he had bees about his mouth. Old Mr.
Spedding showed a courteous contempt, the contempt
of a practical man, for the whole business. "Well,
Mr. FitzGerald," he would say, "and what is it?
Mr. Tennyson reads and Jim criticises, is that it?"

Tennyson refused to visit Wordsworth, although he was constantly reading and quoting from his poems; "I could not get Alfred to Rydal Mount," Spedding wrote. " He would and would not (sulky one), although Wordsworth was hospitably inclined towards him."

Both Spedding and FitzGerald amused themselves by making sketches of Tennyson, and these highly interesting and obviously faithful delineations are reproduced in Lord Tennyson's *Life* of his father. After leaving Mirehouse, FitzGerald and Tennyson went on together to Ambleside, where they stayed a week. FitzGerald thus wrote of his companion to Allen :—

" I will say no more of Tennyson than that the more I have seen of him, the more cause I have to think him great. His little humours and grumpinesses were so droll that I was always laughing : and was often put in mind (strange to say) of my little unknown friend, Undine—I must however say, further, that I felt what Charles Lamb describes, a sense of depression at times from the overshadowing of a so much more lofty intellect than my own : this (though it may seem vain to say so) I never experienced before, though I have often been with much greater intellects : but I could not be mistaken in the universality of his mind ; and perhaps I have received some benefit in the now more distinct consciousness of my dwarfishness."

In July 1835, one Mrs. Short, of Boulge Hall, Woodbridge, died. Mr. John FitzGerald had purchased the property some time before, subject to Mrs. Short's life-interest. He now determined to move to Boulge, and Wherstead, which had been a happy home for ten years, was accordingly relinquished. Boulge Hall is a spacious Queen Anne house, with a fine garden, not far from the White House where FitzGerald was born. He describes it as standing in one of the ugliest and dullest stretches of country in England ; but it

has a compensation in the rich meadow-lands full of
flowers, and the slow stream of the river Deben,
widening to its estuary. Hard by is the flint church
with its brick tower, under the shadow of which
FitzGerald was to be laid to his final rest. About the
same time a friend of his was appointed to the living
of Bredfield. This was George Crabbe the second, son
of the poet, and father of George Crabbe the third, in
whose rectory of Merton in Norfolk FitzGerald was
eventually to die.

Crabbe was a bluff, lovable, sensible man; heroic,
noble-minded, rash in judgment and act, liable to
sudden and violent emotions, and morbidly self-dis-
trustful, though over-confident in the success of causes
near his heart, with simple habits and a Cervantic
humour.

FitzGerald thus describes him in one of the last
letters he wrote :—

". . . If you can easily lay hand on my old Friend George
Crabbe's Life of his Father the Poet, do read his account of a
family Travel from Leicestershire to Suffolk, and the visit
they paid there to your friend Mr. Tovell. You will find it
some dozen pages on in Chapter VI.—a real Dutch Interior,
done with something of the Father's pencil—but quite unin-
tentionally so; my old George rather hating Poetry—as he
called Verse—except Shakespeare, Young's *Night Thoughts*,
and Thomson's *Seasons*; and never having read his Father's
from the time of editing it in 1834 till drawn to them by me
a dozen years after. Not but what he loved and admired his
father in every shape but that."

The old vicar was fond of flowers and trees, and
pleased FitzGerald by crying out, when he heard of
the felling of some oaks by a neighbouring landowner,
"How scandalously they misuse the globe!" He was
just the sort of man, with his oddities and strongly

marked characteristics, to attract FitzGerald. Crabbe
used to pray aloud for his beloved flock, "including
Mary Ann Cuthbert," a person of doubtful reputation.
His daughters were obliged to empty his pockets of all
spare cash for fear of his giving it away to beggars.
He would sit smoking and meditating in a horrible
little room smelling like an inn-parlour, and reeking
with tobacco, which FitzGerald called "the Cobblery,"
from the fact that Mr. Crabbe there patched up his
sermons. The FitzGeralds went in and out of the
house unannounced, and always welcomed. "We
children," wrote one of the younger Miss Crabbes,
"were proud if he [Edward FitzGerald] let any of us
do anything for him, or if we were allowed by our
father or sisters to go and call him in to lunch, but he
was sure not to come if called, though he would come
if not called."

In 1837 FitzGerald, feeling a desire to have a den
of his own, took up his abode in a thatched lodge or
cottage, containing two rooms, standing by the gate
of Boulge Park. Here, with Shakespeare's bust in a
recess, with a cat, a dog, and a parrot called "Beauty
Bob," he began what he called a very pleasant
Robinson Crusoe sort of life. He was waited upon
by an old couple, John Faiers, a labourer on the
estate, a Waterloo veteran, and Mrs. Faiers, a red-
armed, vain, and snuff-taking lady, with a flower-
trimmed bonnet. FitzGerald installed his books and
pictures in the cottage. The place was a scene of
desperate confusion. There were books everywhere;
pictures on easels; music, pipes, sticks, lying on tables
or on the piano. A barrel of beer provided the means
of simple conviviality. Here FitzGerald would sit,
unkempt and unshaven, in dressing-gown and slippers,
or moon about in the garden. He strolled about the

neighbourhood, calling on his friends; sometimes, but rarely, he went to church, noting the toadstools that grew in the chancel; and led a thoroughly indolent life, though with dreams of literary ambition. "He is in a state," wrote Spedding in 1838, "of disgraceful indifference to everything except grass and fresh air. What will become of him in this world?" A picture which he draws of his life at this time to his friend Allen is very delicately touched:—

"Here I live with tolerable content: perhaps with as much as most people arrive at, and what if one were properly grateful one would perhaps call perfect happiness. Here is a glorious sunshiny day: all the morning I read about Nero in Tacitus lying at full length on a bench in the garden: a nightingale singing, and some red anemones eyeing the sun manfully not far off. A funny mixture all this: Nero, and the delicacy of Spring: all very human, however. Then at half-past one lunch on Cambridge cream cheese: then a ride over hill and dale: then spudding up some weeds from the grass: and then coming in, I sit down to write to you, my sister winding red worsted from the back of a chair, and the most delightful little girl in the world chattering incessantly. So runs the world away. You think I live in Epicurean ease: but this happens to be a jolly day: one isn't always well, or tolerably good, the weather is not always clear, nor nightingales singing, nor Tacitus full of pleasant atrocity. But such as life is, I believe I have got hold of a good end of it. . . ."

In the summer FitzGerald generally went off to visit Browne at Bedford, and there spent long days in the open air, rambling about and fishing. His moods were not always serene; with a kind of feminine jealousy which was mingled with his nature he would make snappish and acrimonious retorts to Browne's most innocent remarks, repenting of them moist-eyed, and saying "I hate myself for them." The thought of leaving Browne used to weigh on him for days. "All this must have an end," he wrote, "and, as is usual, my pleasure in Browne's stay is proportionately darkened by the anticipation of his going. . . . Well, Carlyle told us that we are not to expect to be happy."

In this mood he would go to London for distraction, and find himself longing for the country; he wrote to Bernard Barton :—

"A cloud comes over Charlotte Street, and seems as if it were sailing softly on the April wind to fall in a blessed shower upon the lilac buds and thirsty anemones somewhere in Essex : or, who knows? perhaps at Boulge. Out will run Mrs. Faiers, and with red arms and face of woe haul in the struggling windows of the cottage, and make all tight. Beauty Bob will cast a bird's eye out at the shower, and bless the useful wet. Mr. Loder will observe to the farmer for whom he is doing up a dozen of Queen's Heads, that it will be of great use : and the farmer will agree that his young barleys wanted it much. The German Ocean will dimple with innumerable pin points, and porpoises rolling near the surface sneeze with unusual pellets of fresh water—

'Can such things be,
And overcome us like a summer cloud,
Without our special wonder?'"

And again to Frederic Tennyson, after escaping to Boulge :—

"But one finds few in London *serious* men : I mean *serious* even in fun ; with a true purpose and character whatsoever it may be. London melts away all individuality into a common lump of cleverness. I am amazed at the humour and worth and noble feeling in the country, however much railroads have mixed us up with metropolitan civilisation. I can still find the heart of England beating healthily down here, though no one will believe it.

"You know my way of life so well that I need not describe it to you, as it has undergone no change since I saw you. I read of mornings; the same old books over and over again, having no command of new ones : walk with my great black dog of an afternoon, and at evening sit with open windows, up to which China roses climb, with my pipe, while the blackbirds and thrushes begin to rustle bedwards in the garden, and the nightingale to have the neighbourhood to herself. We have had such a spring (bating the last ten days) as would have satisfied even you with warmth. And such verdure ! white clouds moving over the new-fledged tops of oak-trees, and acres of grass striving with buttercups. How old to tell of, how new to see ! "

At this time he made the acquaintance of Samuel Laurence, the portrait-painter, whom he afterwards employed to paint some of his friends' portraits for him; "a dear little fellow," wrote FitzGerald, "a gentleman—made of nature's very finest clay—the most obstinate little man—incorrigible, who wearies out those who wish most to serve him, and so spoils his own fortune."

FitzGerald also found time, if tradition is to be believed, to fall in love with Miss Caroline Crabbe, the daughter of his old friend the Vicar. It is to be wished that this romance had had a normal ending. But it seems that Miss Crabbe was alarmed at Fitz-Gerald's religious views, which were becoming more and more indefinite ; moreover, though FitzGerald was rich enough to dawdle, he was hardly rich enough to support a wife. The girl too was needed at home, being the eldest of a large family ; and she accordingly refused him ; but remained a dear and valued friend, and was one of the party assembled at Merton when FitzGerald died.

CHAPTER II

MIDDLE LIFE

THE years passed slowly and easily, while FitzGerald flitted hither and thither like a great shy moth. Now he is in Dublin with Browne, staying with some Purcell cousins; now he is at Edgeworthstown, sitting in the library, while Miss Maria, neat, dapper, grey-haired, thin and pale, aged seventy-two, sits writing at the table or making a catalogue of her books, quite undisturbed by the general conversation. Now he is in London, getting on very well, as he writes, with his majestic mother, "by help of meeting very little." He goes out a drive with Dickens, Thackeray, and Tennyson, a precious carriage-full. Dickens he finds "unaffected and hospitable," but sees nothing in his face which would indicate genius, except "a certain acute cut of the upper eyelid." Or he would wander farther afield with an old friend. In the company of Tennyson he visited Stratford-on-Avon in 1840. FitzGerald was more moved by the sight of the old footpath to Shottery, so often trodden by Shakespeare, than by the sight of his house or his tomb.

From the year 1842 dates FitzGerald's friendship with Carlyle, or "Gurlyle," as he appears in many of FitzGerald's letters, being so named by Thackeray, who was never content till he had transformed his friends' names into some more conversational form. It appears that Carlyle and Dr. Arnold had visited

the field of Naseby a short time before, in order to
provide accurate materials for Carlyle's *Cromwell*.
Misled by an obelisk erected by FitzGerald's father to
mark the highest ground, which they took to com-
memorate the scene of the hottest engagement, they
had surveyed with complete satisfaction, not the battlefield at all, but a tract of adjacent country, and had
identified, erroneously but without misgiving, all the
recorded topography. The incident casts a lurid light
upon historical research conducted *in situ*. FitzGerald
called upon Carlyle in 1842, under the wing of
Thackeray, and, as the greater part of the battlefield
belonged to his father, was able to enlighten the historian as to the blunder that had been made. Guided
by local tradition, FitzGerald conducted some exca-
vations at Naseby, and found the remains of many
skeletons closely packed together. In the intervals of
his task he read the *Georgics*, and watched the horses
plodding and clanking out to the harvest-fields, up the
lanes with their richly twined tapestries of briony and
bind-weed.

Carlyle was much excited by the discoveries; "the
opening of the burial-heap," he wrote, "blazes strangely
in my thoughts; there are the very jaw-bones that
were clenched together in deadly rage, on this very
ground one hundred and ninety-seven years ago! It
brings the matter home to one, with a strange veracity
—as if for the first time one saw it to be no fable, and
theory, but a dire fact." "Why does the obelisk
stand there ? It might as well stand at Charing Cross ;
the blockhead that it is."

But the task of excavation was not much to Fitz-
Gerald's taste. "I don't care much for all this bone-
rummaging myself," he wrote to Bernard Barton, and
again in the same letter, of the uncovered dead :—

" In the mean time let the full harvest moon wonder at
them as they lie turned up after lying hid 2400 revolutions
of hers.   Think of that warm 14th of June when the Battle
was fought, and they fell pell-mell ; and then the country
people came and buried them so shallow that the stench was
terrible, and the putrid matter oozed over the ground for
several yards ; so that the cattle were observed to eat those
places very close for some years after."

Carlyle desired that a block of stone should be
erected over the grave, bearing the words, " Here, as
proved by strict and not too impious examination, lie
the slain of the Battle of Naseby," but the project was
never carried out.

At this time FitzGerald saw a good deal of a curious
and interesting character, whose religious enthusiasm
made a strong impression on him.   John FitzGerald,
Edward's eldest brother, an eccentric man of great
earnestness, was mainly occupied in evangelistic
work, and not only held services at Boulge, but
made itinerant tours about the country, inspired by
the most fantastic zeal for lecturing his fellow-men
on their duty, and threatening the impenitent with
all the terrors of hell.   He thus became a close
friend of the Rev. Timothy Richard Matthews, originally a clergyman of the Church of England, but at
this time residing at Bedford, and holding services
in a proprietary Chapel.   Matthews was a man of
indomitable energy and primitive faith.   " He believed
in Jesus Christ," wrote FitzGerald, "and had no misgivings whatever."   He often preached in the open
air, in black gown and bands, blowing a trumpet to
attract a crowd   Sometimes he would hold baptismal
services at a reservoir near Naseby, belonging to a
Canal Company, and immerse converts, in company
with John FitzGerald ; or he would anoint the sick

with oil, or pray ineffectually over a deaf person,
putting down the failure to restore hearing to a
deficiency of faith. He was a man of vivid and pithy
talk. "John, be sure you are in the first resurrec-
tion," he said to John Linnet, the vigorous gardener
of the FitzGeralds at Naseby. FitzGerald often
attended his services at Bedford, and hankered regretfully after such unquestioning faith as animated
Matthews. "His sermons," he writes, "shook my
soul." Indeed, under the influence of this fervent
Christian, FitzGerald came as near what is technically
called experiencing religion as his nature admitted.

He wrote:—

"Oh this wonderful wonderful world, and we who stand in
the middle of it are in a maze, except poor Matthews of Bedford, who fixes his eyes upon a wooden Cross and has no
misgiving whatsoever. When I was at his chapel on Good
Friday, he called at the end of his grand sermon on some of
the people to say merely this, that they believed Christ had
redeemed them; and first one got up and in sobs declared
she believed it; and then another, and then another—I was
quite overset—all poor people: how much richer than all who
fill the London Churches."

The pleasant Bedford days were drawing to a
close. Browne became engaged, and in 1844 was
married; he took up his abode at Goldington Hall, two
miles north of Bedford, a house filled with furniture
that had belonged to Mrs. Piozzi. But Goldington,
in spite of forebodings, became a second home to
FitzGerald; and with his easy geniality he made
friends with all the oddities in the neighbourhood,
Mr. Monkhouse, an athletic antiquarian clergyman,
and Captain Addington, who kept innumerable cats
in his Turnpike Cottage.

In 1845 Matthews died suddenly; FitzGerald, returning to Bedford, saw his coffin being carried along the street. John FitzGerald delivered the funeral sermon. He continued for some time to keep up Matthews's work at Bedford, but his sermons were of inordinate length, and he lacked the unction of the true evangelist. Edward was keenly alive to the grotesque side of his brother's character. "I wish my brother wouldn't always be talking about religion," he said; and on one occasion remarked that when his brother wrote D.V. in his letters, with reference to a proposed arrangement, as he habitually did, it only meant "if I happen to be in the humour." It seems indeed as if John FitzGerald's eccentricity verged on insanity; when he preached or even when he listened to sermons, he was accustomed to remove certain articles of dress such as boots and stockings, and put the contents of his pockets on the seat of the pew, in order to make himself quite comfortable. At intervals during the discourse he would whistle shrilly, which was a sign of satisfaction. It would appear that he regarded his brother as a vessel of wrath, yet made no serious attempt to convert him; but in whatever form Edward FitzGerald was touched by religion—and there is no doubt that Matthews brought him as near to revivalism as he was likely to go—the perception of his brother's absurdities made the acceptance of so violent and precise a creed a ludicrous impossibility.

At this time the pivot on which FitzGerald's life turned was the Boulge Cottage. He was fond of inviting Barton and Crabbe there, calling them the wits of Woodbridge; or in his blue serge suit, cut very loose, he would stroll up to the Hall farm, where his friend Mr. Job Smith lived, and smoke a clay pipe in the big kitchen, reading the paper, or holding his protégé, Alfred Smith, the farmer's son, between his knees. He wrote of himself in a strain of exaggerated pettishness to Frederic Tennyson, who had written complaining that Fitzgerald's letters were dull :—

"What is a poor devil to do ? You tell me quite truly that my letters have not two ideas in them, and yet you tell me to write my two ideas as soon as I can. So indeed it is so far easy to write down one's two ideas, if they are not very abstruse ones ; but then what the devil encouragement is it to a poor fellow to expose his nakedness so ?

". . . But you see the original fault in me is that I choose to be in such a place as this at all ; that argues certainly a talent for dullness which no situation nor intercourse of men could much improve. It is true ; I really do like to sit in this doleful place with a good fire, a cat and dog on the rug, and an old woman in the kitchen. This is all my live-stock. The house is yet damp as last year; and the great event of this winter is my putting up a trough round the eaves to carry off the wet. There was discussion whether the trough should be of iron or of zinc : iron dear and lasting ; zinc the reverse. It was decided for iron ; and accordingly iron is put up."

But in 1846 he formed another of his great friendships. This was with E. B. Cowell, afterwards Professor of Sanskrit at Cambridge, then a young man of twenty, son of an Ipswich corn-merchant. Though brought up to business, Cowell had developed an assiduous taste for reading, had learned Latin, Sanskrit, and Persian ; he had finally become engaged to a lady several years older than himself, a Miss Charlesworth, with some small means at her disposal, and married her. Cowell was a shy, modest, humorous man, simple-minded and deeply religious, with an immense and catholic enthusiasm for literature, but with no great gifts of expression. It was he that introduced FitzGerald to Omar Khayyám.

Cowell said humorously of himself that his chief

function was to encourage other people to work. His
great power as a teacher lay in his own enthusiasm,
and also in the fact that his marvellous memory gave
him an extraordinary facility in suggesting parallel
passages and illustrations from a large variety of
authors. "What have you been reading," wrote
FitzGerald to him in 1846, "and what taste of rare
authors have you to send me?"

Cowell's devotion to Sanskrit was such that he
utilised the frequent letters imposed upon him by the
exigencies of courtship as a vehicle for teaching his
fiancée the language, as well as an opportunity of
becoming better acquainted with it himself. He
was now living at a cottage at Bramford, near
Ipswich; and the time that FitzGerald spent there
was probably the happiest of his life. He was as
deeply devoted to Mrs. Cowell as to her husband;
and the three spent many pleasant hours in the cottage
covered with *Pyrus japonica*, with a garden of old-
fashioned flowers, a big monkey-puzzle tree, and a
little footpath leading to the mill. Here they read
Greek, Persian, and Spanish. Mrs. Cowell, with a
green ribbon in her hair, read her poems aloud and
FitzGerald criticised. His memory long after dwelt
upon the smallest details of the scene, though as usual
his pleasure at the time was often over-clouded by the
thought that the sweet days must have a end. The
end came in 1851, when Mrs. Cowell, who had great
ambitions for her husband, decided that he must go
up to Oxford. FitzGerald strongly disapproved of
this; as he wrote to Frederic Tennyson:—

"Not that I think Oxford will be so helpful to his studies
as his counting-house at Ipswich was. However, being
married, he cannot at all events become Fellow, and, as many
do, dissolve all the promise of Scholarship in Sloth, Gluttony,
and sham Dignity."

Mrs. Cowell found it very difficult, in the face of the opposition of FitzGerald and Donne, to carry out her plan; her great ally was a young Mr. George Kitchin, a friend of her husband's, now Dean of Durham. Mrs. Cowell's letters dealing with the matter are full of vigorous humour; her husband showed signs of vacillation.

Mrs. Cowell began by asking FitzGerald to tell Donne that Cowell was going to Oxford, thinking that he would sympathise. Instead of complying, he tried to dissuade Cowell from the intention, saying that all was done and given at Oxford by favour.

"And that he had far better," writes Mrs. Cowell, "try for something (of all *nonsense* to talk) in the wretched Scotch or London Universities. This is never to be thought of. . . . But the mischief of it is that to prove their point they so *distort* College life, in the dreadfully long letters E.F.G. is rousing up his languid energies to send to us, that Edward, who was just beginning, to my heartfelt thankfulness, to *rise* to the occasion, . . . is now almost *wholly* turned back again. . . . E.F.G. may write again, or very probably return here in a day or two. I wrote to try and stop his writing, or using such influence, but *quite* in vain; it only brought on fresh arguments."

She continues, three days afterwards, to Mr. Kitchin:—

"It was beyond measure important that your letter should arrive before another from E.F.G. came, or, what would be worse, himself. . . .

"Edward [Cowell] asks if I have fairly represented E.F.G. and Mr. Donne to you,—perhaps not, but you would *see* that they only meant kindly, and were acting according to their *own* view like true friends, and are both really men of the highest principle, as far as a *man* can be, who doubts if Scripture be altogether the highest guide—and also men of fine taste and real scholarship; but they are men *totally* incapable of appreciating Edward's higher qualities. . . ."

Still, Mrs. Cowell carried her point, and FitzGerald was overwhelmed with unhappiness; he wrote to the Vicar of Bredfield :—

". . . My heart saddens to think of Bramford all desolate; and I shall now almost turn my head away as any road or railroad brings me within sight of the little spire! I write once a week to abuse both of them for going. But they are quite happy at Oxford. . . ."

FitzGerald was at this time trying in a quiet way to make himself useful, not so much on principle, but because it amused him; he used to teach the children in the village school near Boulge; and it was thus that he saw a good deal of Lucy Barton, the daughter of Bernard Barton, who used to teach in the Sunday-schools, and drifted into what seems to have become an indefinite engagement of marriage. In 1849 Bernard Barton died, leaving Miss Barton very ill-provided for. FitzGerald at once took upon himself to edit, with an introduction, a selection from her father's letters and poems, which appeared in the same year. He took great pains to collect subscribers' names, and induced his friends and relations to order a great number of copies. Carlyle, Thackeray and Trench were on the list, while Spedding took ten copies, and George Crabbe no fewer than twelve. FitzGerald appears to have promised Bernard Barton that his daughter should be provided for after his death; and it seems that both Barton and his daughter regarded this as tantamount to an offer of marriage, but that FitzGerald did not so regard it; indeed the affair is involved in a good deal of mystery.

Up to this time life had gone prosperously with FitzGerald, but in the year 1851 he felt the sharp touch of adversity. He had been using his eyes injudiciously, reading till late at night by a dim paraffin lamp, and they began to trouble him. But he employed his disability like the ancient blind philosopher, *puero ut uno esset comitatior*. His protégé, Alfred Smith, the son of the farmer at the Hall farm, was now a big boy, and FitzGerald engaged him to come up in the evenings and read to him. Alfred was the first of a series of readers; FitzGerald made much of the boy, and used to take him up to town to see the sights; but he did not neglect his education, and diligently questioned him about the books they read.

Meanwhile the affairs of FitzGerald's father had been going from bad to worse. He had been sinking all the money he could raise in developing the coal on his Manchester estates, and he had recklessly involved his friend and neighbour, Squire Jenny, in the same hapless enterprise. The unfortunate old man drove one morning to a friend's house, and hurried into his room saying, "I'm in a devil of a mess! I'm ruined!" Mr. FitzGerald's effects at the Hall were sold up. Neither he nor Squire Jenny could rally from the blow, and they both died in the course of the next few months. To meet the claims of the Squire's creditors, the great pleasant woods on his estate were felled. Edward's allowance from his father came to an end; but the greater part of his mother's property was fortunately secured to her, so that any diminution of resources from which he suffered was merely temporary.

FitzGerald called on Miss Barton to tell her of his altered prospects, but renewed the pledge that he had made to her father that she should never be in want. It seems indeed probable that the delicacy which FitzGerald felt about offering Miss Barton a

C

definite money allowance was what eventually pre-
cipitated his resolution to offer her marriage.

After her husband's death, FitzGerald's mother left
the neighbourhood, settling at Richmond. But Fitz-
Gerald made no change in his own habits, except
that in this year he printed a book of extracts which
he called *Polonius: a Collection of Wise Saws and
Modern Instances.* "Not a book of *Beauties*," he described it in his preface, "other than as all who have
the best to tell, have also naturally the best way of
telling it"; nor of the "limbs and outward flourishes
of Truth, however eloquent; but in general, and as far
as I understand, of clear, decided, wholesome and
available insight into our nature and duties. . . . The
grand Truisms of life only life itself is said to bring to
life."

The introduction, which is a little stilted and dis-
jointed, yet contains some fine passages, such as :—

"And why," says the note-book of one *nel mezzo del cammin
di nostra vita*, "does one day linger in my memory? I had
started one fine October morning on a ramble through the
villages that lie beside the Ouse. In high health and cloud-
less spirits, one regret perhaps hanging upon the horizon of
the heart, I walked through Sharnbrook up the hill, and
paused by the church on the summit to look about me. The
sun shone, the clouds flew, the yellow trees shook in the wind,
the river rippled in breadths of light and dark; rooks and
daws wheeled and cawed aloft in the changing spaces of blue
above the spire; the churchyard all still in the sunshine
below."

The book itself consists of extracts from such writers
as Selden, Bacon, Newman, and Carlyle, and illustrates
a graver and more serious view of life than FitzGerald's
somewhat purposeless existence would have suggested.
But the fact was that the lapse of time and the approach

of adversity had cast a shadow upon his epicurean ease,
and he had passed very quickly from a prolonged youth
into a somewhat premature age.

But the pressure of calamity did have one very
practical effect upon FitzGerald ; it threw him, perhaps
for the sake of distraction, into more continuous
literary work that he had hitherto attempted. He
was reading Spanish, which he had begun under the
auspices of Cowell, and he now set to work to translate six of Calderon's plays.

FitzGerald's principle was not to translate so much
as to give a "fine and efficient" equivalent. He "sank,
reduced, altered, and replaced." He tried to catch the
spirit of the original and to produce a piece of literary
work rather than a mere paraphrase. The book was
published in 1853, and was so severely reviewed in the
Athenæum that FitzGerald endeavoured to withdraw it
from circulation. It also received depreciatory notice
in the *Leader*, in an article which it seems probable
was written by G. H. Lewes.

In the meantime the eldest brother, John Fitz-
Gerald, settled at Boulge, and to Edward's pleasure
allowed the timber on the estate to grow luxuriantly.
Nothing was felled or lopped ; hedges grew up strong
and dense, and the whole place became enveloped in a
screen of vegetation. FitzGerald could not, however,
face the close proximity of his brother, and deserted
his cottage, sending his effects to Farlingay Hall, to
which Mr. Job Smith had moved, and where Fitz-
Gerald was now received as a lodger. He wrote to
Carlyle describing his new quarters :—

"I am at present staying with a Farmer in a very pleasant
house near Woodbridge : inhabiting such a room as even you,
I think, would sleep composedly in ; my host a taciturn,
cautious, honest, active man whom I have known all my Life.

He and his wife, a capital housewife, and his Son, who could carry me on his shoulders to Ipswich, and a Maid servant who, as she curtsies of a morning, lets fall the Tea-pot, etc., constitute the household."

But he could not settle down. He drifted about more than ever, staying, for instance, at Bredfield with Crabbe for two months together.

In 1853 FitzGerald took up the study of Persian; Cowell, in the following year, published a translation of the Odes of Hafiz, and FitzGerald worked at Bredfield on a translation of Jami's *Salámán and Absál*, which he published eventually in 1856. He spent some weeks at Oxford in Cowell's company, and there improved his knowledge of the language and literature.

At Farlingay he bought a boat, which shows that his finances were not greatly depleted, and spent many hours in sailing on the Deben in company with *Virgil*, *Juvenal* and Wesley's *Journal*. In the same year he visited Bath, where he met Landor, now in his eightieth year. "(He) has some hundred and fifty Pictures," FitzGerald wrote, "each of which he thinks the finest specimen of the finest Master, and has a long story about how he got it, when, etc. I dare say some are very good; but also some very bad. He appeared to me to judge of them as he does of Books and Men; with a most uncompromising perversity which the Phrenologists must explain to us after his Death."

In 1854 his mother died, and John succeeded to the estates, assuming the additional name of Purcell before FitzGerald.

In the course of the year Carlyle, being overworked, announced his intention of coming to stay with FitzGerald, who looked forward to the visit with

amusement tempered with considerable apprehension.
He begs Mrs. Carlyle to tell him what the Sage is to
eat, drink, and avoid. He makes out elaborate way-
bills for Carlyle, and assures him that he will have
perfect freedom about work and exercise; that he may
smoke when and where he will; and have "a capital
sunshiny airy Bedroom without any noise." "If you
don't find yourself well," he adds, "or at ease with us,
you have really but to go, without any sort of Cere-
mony, as soon as you like."

Carlyle replies in a characteristic strain. "It will be
pleasant," he writes, "to see your face at the end of
my shrieking, mad, (and to me quite horrible) rail
operations." . . . "I hope to get to Farlingay not long
after four o'clock, and have a quiet mutton chop in due
time, and have a ditto pipe or pipes: nay I could even
have a bathe if there was any sea water left in the
evening." The visit went off better than could have
been expected. Carlyle wrote of FitzGerald afterwards as a "lonely, shy, kind-hearted man, who dis-
charged the sacred rites (of hospitality) with a kind of
Irish zeal or piety." His only complaint was that he
was not left quite enough alone; and he was graciously
pleased to observe of FitzGerald's friends that he "did
not fare intolerably with them." The weather was good,
and the sage sat much in the open air, under an elm,
reading. When he departed, he chose the steamer,
declining to be shut up in a railway carriage "like a
great codfish in a hamper." On his return he sent
FitzGerald a new inscription for the Naseby monument,
which was to be signed by FitzGerald, and to end with
the words "Peace henceforth to these old Dead." He
seems to have enjoyed his visit, and wrote, a month
afterwards: "On the whole I say, when you get your
little Suffolk cottage, you must have in it a 'chamber

in the wall' for me, *plus* a pony that can trot, and a
cow that gives good milk; with these outfits we shall
make a pretty rustication now and then, not wholly
Latrappish, but only *half*, on much easier terms than
here; and I for one shall be right willing to come and
try it, I for one party. . . . after the beginning of next
week, I am at Chelsea, and (I dare say) there is a fire in
the evenings now to welcome you there. Show face in
some way or other. And so adieu, for my hour of
riding is at hand."

The serene egotism of this letter is very characteristic; and Carlyle's view of hospitality, that everything
should be arranged for the comfort of the guest concerned, shows the lack of courtesy that differentiates
him so strongly from his host.

In 1856 came a joy and sorrow hand in hand.
Browne, who had been long absent on garrison duty
in Ireland, during the Crimean War, returned to Goldington, "a bloody warrior," as FitzGerald called him.
But the beloved Cowell had also accepted a Professorship of History at Calcutta, and FitzGerald's heart was
heavy. Every detail of the last day he spent with
the Cowells—the scent and stir of the hayfield, the
echo of his own husky voice—dwelt with FitzGerald
for many a day.

FitzGerald could not face the parting with these
dear friends. He wrote:—

"MY DEAR EDWARD AND ELIZABETH COWELL,—I think it
is best for many reasons that I should *not* go to see you again
—to say a Good-Bye that costs me so much.

"I shall very soon write to you; and hope to keep up
something of Communion by such meagre Intercourse. Do
you do the same to me. Farewell, Both! Ever your's,

ED. FITZG."

In the October of the same year FitzGerald met

George Borrow, then living in a lonely house near
Oulton Broad, and busy writing the *Romany Rye*.
FitzGerald found this strange pilgrim's masterful manners and irritable temper uncongenial. Yet he said
long after that he was almost the only friend Borrow
had never quarrelled with.

And then befell what must be considered the greatest
mistake of FitzGerald's life, his marriage to Miss
Barton. It is difficult to realise exactly what the
relations of the pair at this time were. At some period
or other they must have become definitely engaged,
possibly when FitzGerald discovered that he would still
be in comparatively easy circumstances. It is clear,
at all events, that about this time he began to consider
himself pledged to marry Miss Barton ; he wrote, soon
after his marriage, "had good sense and experience
prevailed . . . it would never have been completed !
You know my opinion of a 'Man of Taste,' never so
dangerous as when tied down to daily Life Com-
panionhood." FitzGerald had discussed the matter
with Browne, who foresaw nothing but unhappiness as
the result of this ill-assorted union. "Give her anything
you like but your hand," he said. W. H. Thompson
had also strongly urged him to make an honourable
withdrawal. Indeed Miss Barton herself begged him
to terminate the engagement, if he did not think
the marriage would be for his happiness. But Fitz
Gerald was obstinate, with the obstinacy of a weak
and sensitive nature. He expected no great accession
to his happiness — there was indeed little romance
possible for these middle-aged lovers, both nearer
fifty than forty — and the utmost Fitzgerald seems
to have hoped was that he might be allowed to
continue his easy-going independent life in the
company of one, many of whose qualities he admired.

Probably, like many indecisive people, he did not
know how much his own habits had crystallised.
The marriage took place at Chichester on Novem-
ber 4, 1856; the newly married pair went to
Brighton, and then settled for a time at 31 Great
Portland Street, London. A few days of married life
were enough to disillusionise FitzGerald. He found himself the husband of a kindly, conventional, methodical
woman, who looked forward to her marriage with a
man of comparative wealth and of assured social standing as an opportunity to live a thoroughly ordinary,
commonplace life, with all the customary accompani-
ments of visits and parties. Mrs. FitzGerald wanted
her husband to pay calls, to receive visitors, to dress
for dinner. Perhaps if she had shown greater tact
and sympathy she might have made herself indis-
pensable to her husband's happiness. If she had
realised her position as the wife of an able and somewhat eccentric man, and arranged their life to suit his
requirements, it would have been a contented and
might have been a happy marriage. But it was the
other way; Mrs. FitzGerald had her own theory of
married life, and seems to have thought that she could
influence her husband into conformity. FitzGerald, on
the other hand, was not less to blame; he made no
concessions, no sacrifice of tastes; he held on his way,
and appears to have felt that he might have asserted
himself; but he shrank with horror from the conflict
involved. After a fortnight they separated for five
weeks, her husband joining her at Geldestone; and
again took up their quarters in Portland Terrace,
Regent's Park. FitzGerald sank into the extremest
dejection; writing to Cowell about their parting, he
said: "I believe there are new channels fretted in
my cheeks with many unmanly tears since then";

and again: "Till I see better how we get on, I dare
fix on no place to live or die in." But he worked on
at his Persian, and though he had little heart for work,
he produced a translation of Attar's *Bird Parliament*,
not published till after his death. They lingered on in
London, and in April he received letters from Cowell.
In a vein of hopeless depression he writes:—

"Yours and your wife's dear good Letters put into my
hand as I sit in the sunshine in a little Balcony outside the
Windows looking upon the quite green hedge side of the
Regent's Park. For Green it is thus early, and such weather
as I never remember before at this Season. Well, your Letters,
I say, were put into my hand as I was looking into Æschylus
under an Umbrella, and waiting for Breakfast. My wife cried
a good deal over your wife's Letter I think, I think so. Ah
me! I would not as yet read it, for I was already sad; but
I shall answer hers to me which I did read indeed with many
thoughts."

The ill-assorted pair then tried life in the country,
at Gorleston near Yarmouth, but FitzGerald got no
pleasure except in visits to Browne. At last, after
dismal self-communing, he made up his mind. There
was no definite separation, but after this date Fitz-
Gerald never rejoined his wife, and eventually a liberal
allowance was placed at her disposal. She went to
live at Hastings, then at Croydon. FitzGerald
summed up the situation at a later period:—

"Not less do I thank you sincerely for what you say
than for the kindly reticence you have always shown in the
matter of Mrs. E. F. G. You know well enough, from your
own as well as your husband's knowledge of the case, that
I am very much to blame, both on the score of stupidity in
taking so wrong a step, and want of courageous principle in
not making the best of it when taken. *She* has little to
blame herself for, except in fancying she knew both me and
herself better than I had over and over again told her was

the truth *before* marriage. Well, I won't say more. I think you will admit that she is far better off than she *was*, and as I feel sure, ever *would have been* living with me. She was brought up *to rule* ; and though I believe she would have submitted to be a slave, it would have been at too great a price to her, and I doubt no advantage to me. She can now take her own way, live where she likes, have what society she likes, etc., while every year and every day I am creeping out of the world in my own way."

FitzGerald and his wife sometimes exchanged letters ; but though Mrs. FitzGerald endeavoured to persuade her husband to see her, she never prevailed. She always spoke affectionately of him. Once indeed they met face to face, as will be hereafter related ; but they never interchanged another word. FitzGerald fell back at once, with an extreme sense of relief, into his lonely ways, though deeply annoyed at the criticisms on his action which came to his ears.

To add to his unhappiness, his old friend Crabbe fell ill ; he wrote of it to Cowell :—

"First, however, I must tell you how much ill poor Crabbe has been : a sort of Paralysis, I suppose, in two little fits, which made him think he was sure to die ; but Dr. Beck at present says he may live many years with care. Of this also I shall be able to tell you more before I wind up. The brave old Fellow ! he was quite content to depart, and had his Daughter up to give her his Keys, and tell her where the different wines were laid ! I must also tell you that Borrow is greatly delighted with your MS. of *Omar* which I showed him : delighted at the terseness so unusual in Oriental Verse. But his Eyes are apt to cloud ; and his wife has been obliged, he tells me, to carry off even the little *Omar* out of reach of them for a while. . . ."

The exact circumstances which led to FitzGerald's making acquaintance with the Quatrains of Omar will be related lower down. But the above extract shows

that he was at this time at work upon the translation
of the book, which, after a year's fruitless sojourn in
an editor's drawer, was to see the light in 1859.

But, to resume, in September 1857, his old friend
died at Bredfield. FitzGerald wrote to Crabbe's son,
in a way which showed that he felt a real sympathy
with Mrs. FitzGerald's isolated position. " I want your
sisters so much to go to my wife at Gorleston when
they can. I am convinced that their going to her would
be the very thing for herself, poor soul ; taking her out
of herself, and giving her the very thing she is pining
for, namely, some one to devote herself to." FitzGerald
went to Crabbe's funeral ; and then wandered to
London, where a blow that he had never dreamed of
fell upon him. The beloved Browne, Phidippus, the
gallant horseman, was out hunting on the 28th of
January 1859, when his horse, accidentally touched by
some rider's whip, reared and fell upon him. He was
carried home, and lingered for nine weeks in hopeless
agony, borne gallantly and courageously. FitzGerald
hurried to Goldington, but could not be persuaded
to face an interview with his friend. At last he
overcame the shrinking ; he wrote to Donne from
Goldington :—

" Your folks told you on what Errand I left your house
so abruptly. I was not allowed to see W. B. the day I
came : nor yesterday till 3 P.M. ; when, poor fellow, he tried
to write a line to me, like a child's ! and I went, and
saw, no longer the gay Lad, nor the healthy Man, I had
known : but a wreck of all that : a Face like Charles I.
(after decapitation almost) above the Clothes : and the poor
shattered Body underneath lying as it had lain eight weeks ;
such a case as the Doctor says he had never known. Instead
of the light utterance of other days too, came the slow, painful
syllables in a far lower Key : and when the old familiar words,

'Old Fellow—Fitz.'—etc., came forth, so spoken, I broke down too in spite of foregone Resolution.

"They thought he'd die last Night: but this Morning he is a little better: but no hope. He has spoken of me in the Night, and (if he wishes) I shall go again, provided his Wife and Doctor approve. But it agitates him: and Tears he could not wipe away came to his Eyes. The poor Wife bears up wonderfully."

And again to Mr. Aldis Wright:—

"... I was by his Bedside, where he lay (as for three months he had lain) broken in half almost; yet he looked at me with his old discrimination and said, 'I suppose you have scarce ever been with a dying person before?' He had rare intuition into Men, Matters, and even into Matters of Art: though Thackeray would call him 'Little Browne'—which I told him he was not justified in doing. They are equal now."

On the next day, Sunday, the 27th of March, while waiting for Browne to die, FitzGerald wrote two pathetic inscriptions in the *Godefridus* of Kenelm Digby, and the *Euphranor*, copies of which he had himself given to his friend in the old days.

"This book," ran the first, "I gave my dear W. K. B. about twenty years ago; when then believing it, and believing it *now*, to contain a character of himself (especially at pp. 89, etc.), though he might be the last to negotiate it as his own likeness. I now think his son cannot do better than read it, with the light his father's example sheds upon it."

In the *Euphranor* he wrote, "This little book would never have been written, had I not known my dear friend William Browne, who, unconsciously, supplied the moral."

These sad inscriptions are like the scrawls of some disconsolate prisoner, with the weight of doom lying heavy on his heart.

They had not long to wait.   On the 30th of March
Browne died.

FitzGerald had exhausted the depths of grief ; he
wrote to Cowell :—

". . . I have had a great Loss. W. Browne was fallen
upon and half crushed by his horse near three months ago : and
though the Doctors kept giving hopes while he lay patiently
for two months in a condition no one else could have borne
for a Fortnight, at last they could do no more, nor Nature
neither : and he sunk.   I went to see him before he died—
the comely spirited Boy I had known first seven-and-twenty
years ago—lying all shattered and Death in his Face and
Voice. . . .

" Well, this is so : and there is no more to be said about
it.   It is one of the things that reconcile me to my own
stupid Decline of Life—to the crazy state of the world—
Well—no more about it."

He was sent some little mementoes of Browne ; but
he could not return to Goldington ; and he lay under
the shadow of his loss for many days.

CHAPTER III

In 1860 FitzGerald pitched his moving tent in Woodbridge Market-place, over a gun-maker's shop. He crammed his little rooms with all his books and pictures, and took up again the thread of his lonely life. He was now in flourishing circumstances, as his mother's death had put him in possession of nearly a thousand a year; but the idea of a settled home, which sometimes occurred to him, was overshadowed by the thought of the troubles of housekeeping. He wrote at this date the poem called "Virgil's Garden laid out à la Delille," an idyll which appeared long after in *Temple Bar*. Mr. Job Smith of Farlingay died, and young Alfred settled at a farm called Sutton Hoo, a house just across the river, approached by a ferry. FitzGerald had a small yacht built, which he called *The Scandal*, saying that he named it after the main staple of Woodbridge, and adding that all other possible names had been used up. His skipper was one Thomas Newson, a smart sailor, with a nasal twang, and a head perched on one side, "like a magpie looking in a quart pot," as FitzGerald once said—adding, "He is always smiling, yet the wretched fellow is the father of twins"; in this yacht, which was a great resource to him, he took many cruises, once even going as far as Holland.

He wrote to Cowell :—

46

"My chief Amusement in Life is Boating, on River and Sea. The Country about here is the Cemetery of so many of my oldest Friends: and the petty race of Squires who have succeeded only use the Earth for an *Investment*: cut down every old Tree: level every Violet Bank: and make the old Country of my Youth hideous to me in my Decline. There are fewer Birds to be heard, as fewer Trees for them to resort to. So I get to the Water: where Friends are not buried nor Pathways stopt up: but all is, as the Poets say, as Creation's Dawn beheld. I am happiest going in my little Boat round the Coast to Aldbro', with some Bottled Porter and some Bread and Cheese, and some good rough Soul who works the Boat and chews his Tobacco in peace. An Aldbro' Sailor talking of my Boat said—"She go like a Wiolin, she do!' What a pretty Conceit, is it not? As the Bow slides over the Strings in a liquid Tune. Another man was talking yesterday of a great Storm: 'and, in a moment, all as calm as a Clock.'"

But all this was in the pleasant summer when life went easily. It was far different in the short wet winter days; he wrote to George Crabbe:—

"By the bye, don't let me forget to ask you to bring with you my Persian Dictionary in case you come into these Parts. I read very very little, and get very desultory: but when Winter comes again must take to some dull Study to keep from Suicide, I suppose. The River, the Sea, etc., serve to divert one now."

But death was busy among FitzGerald's circle, and he began to feel the unhappiness of having made so many friends among those older than himself. The sense of the brevity, the swift passage of life, began to haunt him like an obsession. His sister Eleanor, Mrs. Kerrich, died in 1863. "The good die," he wrote to Mrs. Browne, "they sacrifice themselves for others; she never thought of herself, only her children. . . . I will not go to the wretched funeral,

where there are plenty of mourners, but I shall go to
Geldestone when they wish me." Late in the year
Thackeray died, at the age of fifty-two ; and FitzGerald
began to live in the past more than ever, in the good
old days. He still could not forget his wife. He
wrote to Mrs. Browne :—

"The last I heard of Mrs. E. F. G. was that she had gone
to Brighton, where I suppose she finds the greatest number
of 'God's afflicted children,' among whom she proposed to
spend the remainder of her days. Do you hear from her ?"

In 1864 Fitzgerald made up his mind to buy a
little farmhouse near Woodbridge, but he did not at
once take up his residence there. He called it Grange
Farm, but afterwards altered the name to Littlegrange.
In the same year came another great friendship. He
made the acquaintance of a stalwart sailor named
Joseph Fletcher, commonly called Posh. It was at
Lowestoft that he was found, where FitzGerald used,
as he wrote in 1859, "to wander about the shore at
night longing for some fellow to accost me who might
give some promise of filling up a very vacant place
in my heart." Posh had seen the melancholy figure
wandering about, and, years after, when FitzGerald
used to ask him why he had not been merciful enough
to speak to him, Posh would reply that he had not
thought it becoming.

Posh was, in FitzGerald's own words, "a man of the
finest Saxon type, with a complexion *vif, mâle et
flamboyant*, blue eyes, a nose less than Roman, more
than Greek, and strictly auburn hair that any woman
might sigh to possess." He was, too, according to
FitzGerald, "a man of simplicity of soul, justice of
thought, tenderness of nature, a gentleman of Nature's
grandest type." FitzGerald became deeply devoted

to this big-handed, soft-hearted, grave fellow, then twenty-four years of age. FitzGerald thus wrote of him to Laurence :—

"The Great Man . . . is yet there : commanding a Crew of those who prefer being his Men to having command of their own. And they are right ; for the man is Royal, tho' with the faults of ancient Vikings. . . . His Glory is somewhat marred ; but he looks every inch a King in his Lugger now. At home (when he is there, and not at the Tavern) he sits among his Dogs, Cats, Birds, etc., always with a great Dog following abroad, and aboard. This is altogether the Greatest Man I have known."

And again to the same :—

"You will see . . . . a little of his simplicity of Soul ; but not the Justice of Thought, Tenderness of Nature, and all the other good Gifts which make him a Gentleman of Nature's grandest Type."

And again to Spalding : [1]—

"Oh, these [Posh and his wife] are the People who some-how interest me ; and if I were not now too far advanced on the Road to Forgetfulness, I should be sad that my own life had been such a wretched Concern in comparison. But it is too late, even to lament, now. . . ."

And again to the same, of entering a church at Yar-mouth with Posh :—

". . . when Posh pulled off his Cap, and stood erect but not irreverent, I thought he looked as good an Image of the Mould that Man was originally cast in as you may chance to see in the Temple of *the Maker* in these Days. The Artillery were blazing away on the Denes ; and the little Band-master, who played with his Troop here last summer, joined us as we were walking, and told Posh not to lag behind, for he was not at all ashamed to be seen walking with him. The little Well-meaning Ass !

---

[1] Frederick Spalding died 1902, an antiquary and archæolo-gist, curator of the Castle Museum at Colchester ; formerly a neighbour of FitzGerald's at Woodbridge.

It must be confessed that a good deal of sentimentality was wasted over this sea-lion. Nothing
that Posh might do could be criticised. Thus on
on one occasion it is related that Posh, after being
sumptuously feasted at FitzGerald's lodgings, lay down
at full length on the sofa. Mr. Alfred Smith, who
was present, and thought that this was taking a
liberty, remarked upon it. "Poor fellow!" said Fitz-
Gerald, "look how tired he is!" Posh's one failing
was drink, to which he occasionally gave way. But
FitzGerald could not bear to judge him severely; he
wrote to Spalding of one of these lapses :—

"I declare that it makes me feel ashamed very much to
play the Judge on one who stands immeasurably above me
in the scale, whose faults are better than so many virtues.
Was not this very outbreak that of a great genial Boy among
his old Fellows? True, a Promise was broken. Yes, but if
the whole man be of the Royal Blood of Humanity, and do
Justice in the Main, what are the *people* to say?"

Among other kindnesses FitzGerald built a herring-
lugger for Posh, retaining the interest of a partner;
he named it *The Meum and Tuum*; but it did not prove
a successful venture, and it was afterwards made over
to Posh altogether.

But among his diversions FitzGerald did not forget
his literary work: he took up Calderon again and
translated two more plays, *The Mighty Magician* and
Such Stuff as Dreams are made of, which appeared in
1865.

He also began to improve his house, adding rooms
and altering, draining, and planting his five or six
acres. He was difficult to satisfy. He would order a
piece of building to be done, come wandering up, and
presently give orders for its demolition. He cruised
about a good deal, visiting the south coast of England

as far as the Isle of Wight; and planned abbreviations
of big books like *Clarissa Harlowe* and Wesley's *Journal,*
a species of task in which he took a peculiar delight.
But he was full of melancholy moods. Death seemed
"to rise like a wall" against him whichever way he
looked. He wrote to Allen: "When I read Boswell
and other Memoirs now, what presses on me most is—
All these people who talked and acted so busily are
gone." He finished, too, his translation of the
Agamemnon, which he printed in the same year, 1865,
without a title-page, and had bound in an ugly blue
wrapper. "When one has done one's best," he wrote
to Cowell, "one likes to make an end of the matter by
print. . . . I suppose very few people have ever taken
such Pains in Translation as I have."

At this time John FitzGerald was in a condition of
high rhetorical fervour. Wherever he could get an
audience to address he hurried thither. He was the
despair of meetings at which he took the chair,
because the chairman's address invariably consumed
the whole of the evening; and whatever the subject
of the lecturer might be, John FitzGerald spoke
fervently of temperance and the abominations of
Rome. He undressed himself on these occasions more
industriously than ever, hurled grease about and
knocked hats off pegs. "We FitzGeralds are all mad,"
said Edward," "but John is the maddest of the family,
for he does not know it." John gave way to moods
of deep melancholy; put a clock in every room at
Boulge, yet whenever he desired to know the time he
would ring for his valet to tell him. Yet all the while
he continued to live like a man of position and fortune; kept many servants and horses, and criticised his
brother Edward's wardrobe severely. "The difference
between John and me," said FitzGerald, "is this:

John goes and does things that he knows nothing
about—the most unheard-of things—and thinks he's
perfectly right; while if I want to do anything, I go
to some one who understands and get advice, which,
as a rule, to my misfortune, I don't follow."

An old fishmonger called Levi, in Woodbridge, used
to inquire affectionately after John FitzGerald whenever Edward entered the shop, "And how is the
General, bless him?" "How many times," Fitzgerald
used to say, "Mr. Levi, must I tell you that my
brother is not a General, and was never in the Army?"
"Ah, well, it's my mistake, no doubt! But, anyhow,
bless him!"

FitzGerald was much delighted with his friend
Thompson's appointment to the Mastership of Trinity
in 1866, and wrote to Allen :—

"I have written to congratulate him in a sober way on his
Honours; for, at our Time of Life, I think exultation would
be unseasonable on either side. He will make a magnanimous
Master, I believe; doing all the Honours of his Station well,
if he have health."

In the same year Cowell returned from India on
furlough; but FitzGerald, with a shy perversity,
seemed unable to take up the old relations; he wrote
to Cowell :—

"This time ten years—a month ago—we were all lounging
about in a hayfield before your Mother's House at Rushmere.
I do not forget these things: nor cease to remember them
with a sincere, sad, and affectionate interest: the very
sincerity of which prevents me from attempting to recreate
them. This I wish you and yours, who have been so kind to
me, to believe."

But in 1867, to FitzGerald's great delight, Cowell
obtained the Professorship of Sanskrit at Cambridge,
and the old intercourse was gradually resumed.

FitzGerald cruised a good deal in the summer of 1867 ; but his definite rambles grew fewer ; he came to love his fireside and his own lonely leisurely ways more and more. "I run home like a beaten dog," he said, speaking of his brief visits to other parts of England.

It was at this time that FitzGerald, walking briskly with Posh in Woodbridge Thoroughfare, saw a female form drawing near and a glove being removed. "It's my wife!" said FitzGerald in a tone of tremulous excitement. They met, exchanged looks, held out their hands, but FitzGerald's courage failed at the last moment, and withdrawing his hand he said: "Come along, Posh," and stalked away.

From this time dates FitzGerald's close friendship with Mr. Aldis Wright, his biographer and editor; the occasion being that Dr. Thompson, the Master of Trinity, expressed a wish to have FitzGerald's works in the University Library, and it fell to Mr. Aldis Wright to carry out the desire.

In 1868 came out the second edition of the *Omar*. At this time FitzGerald was also occupied in a task, which to him was a perpetual delight, of rescuing racy terms of local or nautical origin from obscurity. He seems to have had that peculiar pleasure in the outward physiognomy of words, words with old and far-off traditions, or words that grew, as it were, out of the soil, expressive, racy, vernacular phrases. He used to send them to the *East Anglian*. Many of them were drawn from the talk of Posh, and FitzGerald, with the sensitive feeling, so characteristic of him, which led him to credit others with his own sensibilities, carefully concealed from Posh that he made any public use of these words. One day, however, he handed Posh by mistake a proof of one of these contributions to light his pipe

with. Posh began to read the paper, and FitzGerald,
realising his mistake, said: "Well, is that wrong?"
"I don't see but it's all right enough, sir," said Posh
with ready tact. "With perfect unconsciousness,"
said FitzGerald, in relating the incident to W. F.
Pollock, adding maliciously: "In this he differs from
the Laureate."

In 1870 FitzGerald had Posh's portrait painted by
Samuel Laurence, that it might hang side by side with
the same artist's portraits of Tennyson and Thackeray,
as his three greatest friends,—but Posh was the greatest.

In the same year FitzGerald parted with the *Meum
and Tuum* to Posh, who thus became sole owner, and
celebrated the occasion by a great bout of conviviality.
"Keep from the drink, there's a dear fellow," Fitz-
Gerald wrote to him. He induced Posh to sign the
pledge, but after breaking down, Posh refused to renew
it. FitzGerald comforted himself by thinking what
Carlyle had said about great men's faults, and seems
to have considered Posh, if anything, rather nobler
than before.

In 1871, reaching his grand climacteric, FitzGerald
felt a diminution of vitality; he parted with his boat;
he made his will; and finding his eyes trouble him, he
had recourse again to boy readers.

In 1872 he had a visit from Frederic Tennyson, who
was then deeply interested in spiritualistic phenomena.
FitzGerald took Posh to Lowestoft, and they went
together to see the *Merchant of Venice*, Posh sleeping
soundly through the performance. In the next year
began a correspondence with Professor C. E. Norton;
and through him arrived a letter from Ruskin praising
the *Omar Khayyám*, which had remained ten years in
the hand of Burne-Jones, to whom Ruskin had en-
trusted it; a curious voice out of the past. At the

end of the year FitzGerald was forced to move from
his Woodbridge lodgings.   Mr. Berry, his landlord,
became engaged to marry a widow.   FitzGerald, who
was fond of smoking and chatting with Berry in the
evenings, did not relish the introduction of the new
element, and said rather caustically that "old Berry
would now have to be called 'Old Gooseberry.'"   This
rash witticism was repeated to the widow; and the
upshot was that Berry gave him notice to quit.   Berry
did not like the task of breaking with his old friend
and lodger, and came cautiously upstairs to announce
the decision.   His helpmeet, fearing that his courage
might give way, remained at the bottom of the stairs
calling out: "Be firm, Berry!   Remind him of what he
called you."

FitzGerald seems to have had an invincible objection
to occupying his own house; accordingly, on being
ejected, he hired another room in an adjacent house,
where he transferred his Penates.   But he was losing
his zest for life.   In 1874 he wrote that he was beginning to have warnings of the end: "I find life little
worth now; not that I am unhappy, but so wofully
indifferent."

At last, however, he installed himself in his own
house, Littlegrange; but he would only inhabit one
room, a large downstairs parlour, which he divided by
folding-doors.   The living-room was full of books, with
a high-standing desk.   In the hall close by stood an
organ on which he often played, always from memory,
drawing out of it a great richness of melody, and
crooning an air himself as the excitement grew.

He furnished the rest of the house with some care and
dignity, and left it for the use of his nieces, whenever
they chose to visit him; but even when they were in
the house, he was little with them; he took his meals

alone; and sometimes for days together only saw them
for a few minutes in the garden, where he would saunter
along a winding shrubbery walk, with his plaid about
him, wearing blue glasses, and a shade over his eyes,
which were often painful. He would often be heard
humming over to himself old songs in his weak, true
voice. Sunday afternoons he would spend with Alfred
Smith at Sutton Hoo, in an arbour, sipping a glass of
wine and talking of the old days. He consulted a
doctor about this time, who told him that his heart was
affected. This was good news to FitzGerald, who
manifested singular cheerfulness at the announcement,
as holding out to him a prospect of the sudden death
which he desired. In the same year Spedding finished
his monumental edition of Bacon, the fourteenth volume
appearing at that date (1874). "I always look upon
old Spedding's as one of the most wasted lives I know,"
said FitzGerald cheerfully, adding that Spedding had
only succeeded in establishing that view of Bacon's
character which he set out to dissipate.

In the same year FitzGerald paid a pilgrimage to
Abbotsford, and found himself full of emotion; but he
could now less and less bear to be away from home,
and hurried back to Littlegrange after three days.

One of FitzGerald's chief correspondents at this
time was Fanny Kemble, whom he sincerely loved,
though he confessed he did not care for her acting.
She was a lively, witty, vivacious woman, with a tender
heart; she wrote in 1875 some reminiscences of Fitz-
Gerald and others, which appeared in the *Atlantic
Monthly*, but they were couched in so eulogistic a style
that FitzGerald felt bound to paste a piece of paper,
in his own copy, over the passage which concerned
himself. His letters to her, tender, fanciful, affectionate, are among the best he wrote.

In 1876 Tennyson appeared at Woodbridge with his son Hallam. FitzGerald, who had not seen his old friend for twenty years, was characteristically pleased to find that the son called his father "Papa," and not "Governor." Thinking that his visitors would not be comfortable at Littlegrange, he installed them at the Bull Inn. They revived old memories, and Fitz-Gerald took occasion to tell Tennyson that he had better not have written anything after 1842, adding that he had ceased to be a poet, and had become an artist, a remark which Tennyson seems to have taken in good part. It is amusing to note that in the course of the evening they spent together FitzGerald uttered some pieces of local gossip which he thought indiscreet, for he said to Tennyson gravely: "Don't let this go to the Bull."

Tennyson seems to have been much struck by the picture presented by FitzGerald, who sat talking under a tree, with his hair moving in the wind, and his pigeons alighting on his hand or shoulder, curtseying or cooing, and he embodied the scene in the Dedication to his *Tiresias* volume, which FitzGerald did not live to see :—

> " OLD FITZ, who from your suburb grange,
> 　　Where once I tarried for a while,
> Glance at the wheeling Orb of change,
> 　　And greet it with a kindly smile ;
> Whom yet I see as there you sit
> 　　Beneath your sheltering garden-tree,
> And while your doves about you flit,
> 　　And plant on shoulder, hand, and knee,
> Or on your head their rosy feet,
> 　　As if they knew your diet spares
> Whatever moved in that full sheet,
> 　　Let down to Peter at his prayers ;
> Who live on milk and meal and grass."

In 1877 and 1878 FitzGerald amused himself by contributing local notes to the *Ipswich Journal*, signing them Effigy, which stood for E. F. G. But shadows fell across the peaceful path. In 1877 one of his old friends, a boatman named West, died ; and Fitz-Gerald could no longer bear the pleasant reaches of the Deben, where they had so often sailed together. A nephew too died, Maurice, the son of John FitzGerald, a young man of some literary promise, who had published a version of the Hippolytus, but with family irresolution had failed to make the most of his gifts.

In 1878 he drew up and printed a Chronology of the life of Charles Lamb. "I drew it up for myself," he writes, "because I often find myself puzzled about the dates in the dear fellow's life." Pollock called the book "Côtelette d'Agneau à la Minute," and the name pleased FitzGerald; he himself naming it "Some Stepping-stones in dear Charles Lamb."

In 1879 *Omar* appeared again in the fourth edition, bound up with *Salámán and Absál*. And in the same year FitzGerald brought out his little book, *Readings from Crabbe*, with an introduction. He was pleased with the book, and thought it "very dexterously " done.

"Then—my Crabbe is printing—Hurrah, Boys !" he wrote to Pollock.

The writings of Crabbe had always possessed a great fascination for FitzGerald. The cause of this is not far to seek. FitzGerald had the strong perception of the beauty and interest of ordinary and homely life which Crabbe felt so strongly. FitzGerald found himself too in harmony with one who tried to see life steadily, without either disguising or improving it. Then, too, Crabbe's aromatic humour pleased him, a humour which was not inconsistent with a strong sense of the pathos and sadness of life; and here again FitzGerald was in tune with the poet. Even the very artlessness of Crabbe, which led to his being called "Pope in worsted stockings," pleased FitzGerald; he says in the little introduction which he published to his selection from the *Tales of the Hall*, that the book "shares with the Poet's other works in the characteristic disregard of form and diction—of all indeed that is now called 'Art.'" FitzGerald had indeed little sympathy with the modern claims of art. The view which would make of art a kind of holy and solemn creed, an esoteric and mystical initiation, preaching the duty of "self-effectuation" for the artist —this was instinctively repugnant to FitzGerald. He quotes with approval Scott's breezy dictum that he did not care a curse for what he wrote. The brotherhood of art, with its difficult secrets, its consecration, its vocation would have seemed to FitzGerald little better than nonsense. His view rather was that one who loved beauty and man might speak, as simply and directly as he could, without undue care for stateliness and propriety of expression, of what was in his heart. This was his own way and this was Crabbe's way.

In his old age, FitzGerald found himself loving the *Tales of the Hall* better than the earlier work, with its more bitter and saturnine flavour. He says, quoting Sir Walter Scott, that "its characters look back with a kind of humorous retrospect over their own lives, cheerfully extending to others the same kindly indulgence which they solicit for themselves." "The book, if I mistake not," he goes on, "deals rather with the follies than with the vices of men, with the comedy rather than with the tragedy of life. And even the more sombre subjects of the book are relieved by the colloquial intercourse of the narrators, which twines about every story, and, letting in occasional glimpses of the country round, encircles them all with something of dramatic unity and interest, insomuch that of all the Poet's works this one alone does not leave a more or less melancholy impression upon me ; and, as I am myself more than old enough to love the sunny side of the wall, is on that account, I do not say the best, but certainly that which I like best of all his numerous offspring."

FitzGerald treats Crabbe as he was inclined to treat all his favourites ; in some cases he transposes Crabbe's narrative to make it clearer ; and it seems that he must have amused himself by making marginal alterations in his own copy, of expressions which seemed to him to be faulty ; for he apologises for the possible intrusion of such alterations into the text. "Any poetaster," he adds, "can amend many a careless expression which blemishes a passage that none but a poet could indite."

He is well aware of the fact that Crabbe is a poet the effect of whose verse can hardly be seen in selections. The true impression of Crabbe would result, he says, "from being, as it were, soaked in through the longer process by which the man's peculiar genius works."

Two other points probably drew FitzGerald to Crabbe. They both of them had a rich store of sentiment and a capacity for "falling in love," so to speak, with people ; indeed in Crabbe's case this led to some inconvenient and undignified philandering in his old age ; but the cause was the same ; they both felt the same intimate and almost passionate interest in humanity which made them minute and tender observers of men.

Then too, and in FitzGerald's case this must not be neglected—there was the family link, constituted by FitzGerald's close friendship with the son and the grandson of the poet.   FitzGerald started with a predisposition to admire the work of those he loved, not only for its intrinsic merits, but because it was a part of them.   His own feeling about the little book was as follows : he wrote to Mrs. Kemble :—

"You can tell me if you will—and I wish you would— whether I had better keep the little *Opus* to ourselves, or let it take its chance of getting a few readers in public.   You may tell me this very plainly, I am sure ; and I shall be quite as well pleased to keep it unpublished.   It is only a very, very, little Job, you see : requiring only a little Taste and Tact : and if they have failed me—*Voilà!*   I had some pleasure in doing my little work very dexterously, I thought ; and I did wish to draw a few readers to one of my favourite Books which nobody reads.   And, now that I look over it, I fancy that I have missed my aim—only that my Friends will like, etc."

In the same year, 1879, FitzGerald's elder brother died, of a painful disorder, after great suffering. Edward could not bring himself to attend the funeral. The estates of Boulge and Irwell were sold, the only surviving son of John, Gerald, dying a month after his father.

Occasionally FitzGerald slipped up to London ; there is a charming vignette at this time :—

". . . When I was in London, I went to morning Service in Westminster Abbey ; and, as I sat in the Poet's Corner Transept, I looked down for the stone that covers the remains of Charles Dickens, but it may have been covered by the worshippers there.   I had not been inside that Abbey for twenty years, I believe ; and it seemed very grand to me ; and the old Organ rolled and swam with the Boys' voices on the Top through the fretted vault, as you know.   Except *that*, I heard no music, and saw no Sights, save in the Streets."

FitzGerald's country solitude was cheered by visits from Charles Keene, the great black-and-white artist, and other friends. Charles Keene had been a school-fellow of Cowell's at Ipswich. He was a shy creature, brightening up among friends, abstemious, fond of music, fond of old English books; he liked untidiness and tobacco smoke, and was careless about his dress —in every way a congenial companion for FitzGerald.

In December another of the FitzGerald family circle died, his sister, Mrs. De Soyres, leaving only Edward and Mrs. Wilkinson. Long years before he had told Tennyson of her engagement, saying that his sister was about to marry "a Mr. Wilkinson, a clergyman." Tennyson had seized upon the fact that the words made a line of blank verse, and aptly illustrated Wordsworth's weakest manner. He and FitzGerald used laughingly to dispute the ownership of the line.

In 1880 FitzGerald found in an old portfolio a little paper on the *Black Horse* inn and mill of Baldock, which he had written twenty-three years before; and this he now published in *Temple Bar*; he was a good deal at Lowestoft this year with the Cowells, Mr. Aldis Wright, and the faithful Posh; and he visited Crabbe (the third) at his Rectory of Merton. FitzGerald was restless, melancholy, and dissatisfied; his health grew worse, and the disease of the heart made progress. But he was not inactive. He took out his versions of the two plays of Œdipus, which he had practically completed twenty-four years before, and printed them in two parts, issuing only fifty copies of each.

Carlyle died in 1881, and in the following month James Spedding was run over by a cab, and carried hopelessly injured to St. George's Hospital. Spedding

died like a Christian and a philosopher, only expressing
a wish that the cab had done its work more thoroughly.
"I have not known," FitzGerald wrote to Spedding's
niece, "no, nor heard of, any mortal so prepared to
step unchanged into the better world we are promised."

In the summer of 1881 FitzGerald went to Cambridge to see the Cowells, then living in Scroop Terrace. He went to see Mr. Aldis Wright, and felt at
home in his book-lined rooms.

In the winter he was at Woodbridge again.

". . . I suppose that you in Jersey have had no winter yet ;
for even here thrushes pipe a little, anemones make a pale
show, and I can sit in my indoor clothing on a Bench without,
so long as the Sun shines. I can read but little, and count of
my Boy's coming at Night, to read Sir Walter Scott, or some
Travel or Biography, that amuses him as well as me. We are
now beginning the *Fortunes of Nigel*, which I had not expected to care for, and shall possibly weary of before it ends ;
but the outset is nothing less than *delightful* to me. I think
that Miss Austen, George Eliot and Co. have not yet quite
extinguished him, in his later lights."

In 1882 he went to London and saw his old friend
Donne, who lay dying, and the Kembles. "Donne,"
he said tenderly, "ah, there is a man without a fault—
the least selfish man I ever knew."

He wrote sadly to Mr. Aldis Wright :—

". . . My dear Donne was given over by the Doctor some
ten days ago ; but has since rallied—to go through the trial
again ! "

FitzGerald always classed Donne and Spedding
together as two men of great abilities and profound
minds who, in spite of leading laborious lives, had produced results so little commensurate with their powers.

FitzGerald's thoughts in these last years turned
much to the pleasant haunts of his youth, and he

made a farewell pilgrimage to Aldeburgh. "There is
no sea like the Aldeburgh sea," he said to Alfred Smith,
as they paced the beach. "It talks to me." He was
feeling the approaches of age.

". . . I have not yet quite lost my Cold, and you know
how one used to hear that so it was with Old Age : and now
we find it so. Now the Sun shows his honest face I get more
abroad, and have been sitting out under his blessed rays this
very day, which People tell me is quite indiscreet. But I do
not find the breath from Heaven direct nearly so trying as
through a Keyhole."

". . . I am better off than many—if not most—of my
contemporaries ; and there is not much [worth] living for
after seventy-four."

A little honour fell to him this year which pleased
him. The Spanish Ambassador sent him the Calderon
Gold Medal in recognition of his translations.

He got through the winter without any return of
the bronchial troubles that had of late threatened him
in the cold weather. But he felt his end approaching.
"We none of us get beyond seventy-five," he said
to a friend ; and he often spoke of "smelling the
ground," as the sailors say of a ship in shoaling
water. He made his will very carefully, and he packed
his unpublished books in a tin box, with a letter
addressed to Mr. Aldis Wright, expecting and indeed
hoping that his end would be a sudden one. He began
to disperse his books and pictures, sending Mrs.
Tennyson Laurence's portrait of Tennyson. He stole
up to London to see Carlyle's statue and the house in
Cheyne Row, and fell to weeping.

But he could still be merry ; a friend records that
as he sat with FitzGerald in May 1883 at Woodbridge,
on a bench beside the river, FitzGerald called out to
a small boy wading in the ooze, "Little boy, did you

never hear tell of the fate of the Master of Ravenswood?" and then he told the child the story.

He received, too, a visit from an old friend, Archdeacon Groome, a lover of music, who talked to him about the famous singers they had heard in their youth, and made FitzGerald laugh very heartily by imitating Vaughan's singing.

On the 13th of June 1883, he set off for Merton Rectory, taking with him a book or two, into the leaves of which he slipped some bank-notes, as was his wont, for current expenses. The day before he set off he wrote to his friend Laurence. It was the last letter he was ever to write:—

"My dear Laurence,—It is very kind of you to remember one who does so little to remind you of himself. Your drawing of Allen always seemed to me excellent, for which reason it was that I thought his Wife should have it, as being the Record of her husband in his younger days. So of the portrait of Tennyson which I gave his Wife. Not that I did not value them myself, but because I did value them, as the most agreeable Portraits I knew of the two men; and, for that very reason, presented them to those whom they were naturally dearer to than even to myself. I have never liked any Portrait of Tennyson since he grew a Beard; Allen, I suppose, has kept out of that.

"If I do not write, it is because I have absolutely nothing to tell you that you have not known for the last twenty years. Here I live still, reading, and being read to, part of my time; walking abroad three or four times a day, or night, in spite of wakening a Bronchitis, which has lodged like the household 'Brownie' within; pottering about my Garden (as I have just been doing) and snipping off dead Roses like Miss Tox; and now and then a visit to the neighbouring Seaside, and a splash to Sea in one of the Boats. I never see a new Picture, nor hear a note of Music except when I drum out some old Tune in Winter on an Organ, which might almost be carried about the Streets with a handle to turn, and a Monkey on the top of it. So I go on, living a life far too comfortable as compared with that of better, and wiser men : but ever expecting a reverse in health such as my seventy-five years are subject to. What a tragedy is that of —— ! So brisk, bright, good, a little woman, who seemed made to live ! And now the Doctors allot her but two years longer at most, and her friends think that a year will see the End ! and poor ——, tender, true, and brave ! His letters to me are quite fine in telling about it. Mrs. Kemble wrote me word some two or three months ago that he was looking very old : no wonder. I am told that she keeps up her Spirits the better of the two. Ah, Providence might have spared *pauvre et triste Humanité* that Trial, together with a few others which (one would think) would have made no difference to its Supremacy. ' *Voilà ma petite protestation respectueuse à la Providence,*' as Madame de Sévigné says.

"To-morrow I am going (for my one annual Visit) to G. Crabbe's, where I am to meet his Sisters, and talk over old Bredfield Vicarage days. Two of my eight Nieces are now with me here in my house, for a two months' visit, I suppose and hope. And I think this is all I have to tell you of.—Yours ever sincerely,   E. F. G."

He travelled by Bury, and went to look at the old school. He was met at the station by the Rector and driven to the Rectory. He talked cheerfully about Bury at tea, and walked in the garden. But the journey had tired him, and he went to bed at ten o'clock. How his end came to him is not known ; but when a servant went to call him in the morning of June 14th, he gave no answer, and it was found that he had died quietly in the night, as he had desired to die.

His body was taken to Littlegrange, and he was buried beneath the church tower at Boulge, with the words on his tomb that Cowell had taught him to love :—

"It is He that hath made us, and not we ourselves."

Mrs. FitzGerald survived him for fifteen years, and died (1898) at a great age at her house at Croydon.

CHAPTER II

FRIENDS

IT may be admitted that FitzGerald's fame partly depends upon the accident of his having been the chosen friend of several remarkable men. But even allowing his close contact with such memorable personalities as Tennyson, Carlyle, Thackeray; and Spedding to have been accidental, the qualities which made it possible for him to win and retain so warm, so supreme a regard from them were far from accidental. To those whom he loved, even after long absences, he was always the same; though in the case of Cowell he experienced a certain difficulty in taking up the old friendship again on the same terms after his friend's long absence in India.

This devotion was not inconsistent in FitzGerald's case with an extreme clear-sightedness as to the character of his friends. He admired them generously; but he also took severe account of their faults and foibles. Nor did he ever attempt to slur over the amiable weaknesses he discerned. He did not think a friend a poet because, as in the case of Bernard Barton, he happened to write verses, or an artist, because, like Edwards, he painted pictures.

Another remarkable trait in FitzGerald's behaviour to his friends is that no matter how great or famous they became, there was never the least symptom of deference or conscious inferiority in FitzGerald's

67

attitude, though perhaps we may discern faint traces of a mild envy. If he avoided, as he sometimes seemed to do, the society of his more distinguished friends, it was not that he felt on terms of inequality, but that he was morbidly afraid of being involved in their extended social circle.

The friends to whom FitzGerald was most devotedly attached were probably W. K. Browne, Archdeacon Allen, Frederic Tennyson, and Mr. Aldis Wright; and to these he displayed the greatest tenderness and fidelity; but it will be worth while to trace a little more in detail his relations with the four still more famous friends, Tennyson, Carlyle, Thackeray, and Spedding; for these friendships exhibit FitzGerald in the clearest light, and show how strong his critical power was.

FitzGerald began by having an overwhelming admiration for Tennyson both as a poet and a man. He gave Mrs. Kemble the following interesting description of his early appearance in undergraduate days :—

"At that time he looked something like Hyperion shorn of his Beams in Keats's Poem : with a Pipe in his mouth. Afterwards he got a touch, I used to say, of Haydon's Lazarus."

But the early relations between the two are finely exemplified in the following letter, which FitzGerald wrote to Tennyson in 1835 :—

"I have heard you sometimes say that you are bound by the want of such and such a sum, and I vow to the Lord that I could not have a greater pleasure than transferring it to you on such occasions ; I should not dare to say such a thing to a small man, but you are not such a small man assuredly ; and even if you do not make use of my offer, you will not be offended, but put it to the right account. It is very difficult to persuade people in this world that one can part from a bank-note without a pang. It is one of the most simple things I have ever done to talk thus to you, I believe ; but here is an end, and be charitable to me."

FitzGerald saw, probably more clearly than any one, the extraordinary originality and genius which Tennyson displayed by flashes in his ordinary talk. He made a collection of these dicta in a note-book, but though the volume was lost, FitzGerald retained many small reminiscences in his mind, and several of them are given in the *Life* of the poet. Thus, writing to Professor Norton, in 1876, he said :—

"Dante's face I have not seen these ten years : only his Back on my Book Shelf. What Mr. Lowell says of him recalled to me what Tennyson said to me some thirty-five or forty years ago. We were stopping before a shop in Regent Street where were two Figures of Dante and Goethe. I (I suppose) said, 'What is there in old Dante's Face that is missing in Goethe's ?' And Tennyson (whose Profile then had certainly a remarkable likeness to Dante's) said : 'The Divine.'"

FitzGerald welcomed the early poems of Tennyson with a rapturous enthusiasm, kindled by the sweet and generous sympathies of youth, rather than based upon critical appreciation. But his judgment confirmed what his heart suggested. He saw, perhaps as clearly as they could be seen, the pure beauty, the noble originality of Tennyson's first lyrics.

But the sky gradually clouded over. The two drew apart so far as physical propinquity went, and a slow change passed over FitzGerald's view of Tennyson's powers, and the use he was making of them. His view was hardly that the later works were not in themselves beautiful, but he had set his heart on Tennyson producing some colossal monumental work of an epical kind. He had hoped to see him concentrate all his powers to some such poem, and he was distressed to find him becoming, as he thought, diffuse and senti- mental. The *Idylls* disappointed him, because he did not care for epics of chivalry, and disliked the episodical handling of the subject.

Slowly the disapproval increased, and though per- haps FitzGerald was unfair to the later work, yet his verdict will not improbably be re-echoed by future critics : namely, that on Tennyson's early work lies, so to speak, the dew of the morning ; and that the great vogue he enjoyed, coupled with advancing years, the seductive influences of widespread popularity, and possibly even more material considerations, did effect a certain change in his power of conception though not in his technical skill.

Thus FitzGerald wrote to Frederic Tennyson in 1850, that none of the songs inserted between the cantos of *The Princess* had "the old champagne flavour"; and very soon, in a peevish fashion, he lost faith in Tenny- son altogether, and began to rail at, or rather moan over, each of his successive productions in turn. He spoke his mind quite plainly about it to the friends of the poet, and even to the poet himself. Thus he wrote to Frederic Tennyson in 1850 :—

"You know Alfred himself never writes, nor indeed cares a halfpenny about one, though he is very well satisfied to see one when one falls in his way. You will think I have a spite against him for some neglect, when I say this, and say besides that I cannot care for his *In Memoriam*. Not so, if I know myself : I always thought the same of him, and was just as well satisfied with it as now. His poem I never did greatly affect : nor can I learn to do so : it is full of finest things, but it is monotonous, and has that air of being evolved by a Poetical Machine of the highest order. So it seems to be with him now, at least to me, the Impetus, the Lyrical œstrus, is gone. . . . It is the cursed inactivity (very pleasant

to me who am no Hero) of this 19th century which has spoiled
Alfred, I mean spoiled him for the great work he ought now
to be entering upon ; the lovely and noble things he has done
must remain. It is dangerous work this prophesying about
great Men. . . ."

As the years went on, FitzGerald began to feel
more and more that the poet was being lost in the
artist, and that the artist "had not the wherewithal
to work on."   He felt with Carlyle that somehow or
other the great vigour, the splendid fighting qualities of
Tennyson, had not found expression either in thought
or life. He thought that the poet was being "suffocated
by London adulation," and that he was parting with
originality, freshness, and sincerity of aim.   "He has
lost," he wrote, "that which caused the long roll of
the Lincolnshire wave to reverberate in Locksley
Hall."

Though he could even so make some generous allowance :—"pure, lofty, and noble as he always is," he
wrote, near the end of his life, with a flash of the old
admiration.

Perhaps his most deliberate judgment on Tennyson
occurs in a letter to Mrs. Kemble, where he touches
with a firm hand the weak point in Tennyson's life ;
—the weak point, indeed, in FitzGerald's own life—
the self-absorption born of seclusion, and the want
of practical activity telling on a temperament whose
melancholy demanded a certain healthy objectivity
never attained. He is speaking of "Posh," and continues :—

"I thought that both Tennyson and Thackeray were
inferior to him in respect of Thinking of Themselves.   When
Tennyson was telling me of how the *Quarterly* abused him
(humorously, too), and desirous of knowing why one did not
care for his later works, etc., I thought that if he had lived

an active Life, as Scott and Shakespeare ; or even ridden, shot, drunk, and played the Devil, as Byron, he would have done much more, and talked about it much less. 'You know,' said Scott to Lockhart, 'that I don't care a Curse about what I write,' and one sees he did not. I don't believe it was far otherwise with Shakespeare. Even old Wordsworth, wrapped up in his Mountain mists, and proud as he was, was above all this vain Disquietude : proud, not vain, was he : and that a Great Man (as Dante) has some right to be—but not to care what the Coteries say. What a Rigmarole !"

And yet the personal regard remained undimmed and unabated. Year after year FitzGerald kept in touch with the poet and his family circle by whimsical, delicate, loving letters; and Tennyson, too, when asked at the end of his life which of his friends he had loved the best, would reply unhesitatingly, "Why, old Fitz, to be sure !"

FitzGerald's personal acquaintance with Carlyle began in 1842 when Thackeray, or, according to another account, Samuel Laurence, took him to tea in Carlyle's house. Their friendship ripened over the exploration of Naseby Field, and in 1846 they were writing to each other as "Dear Carlyle" and "Dear FitzGerald."

The following is a little account of a visit he paid Carlyle in 1844 :—

"I smoked a pipe with Carlyle yesterday. We ascended from his dining-room carrying pipes and tobacco up through two stories of his house, and got into a little dressing-room near the roof : there we sat down : the window was open, and looked out on nursery gardens, their almond trees in blossom, and beyond, bare walls of houses, and over these, roofs and chimneys, and roofs and chimneys, and here and there a steeple, and whole London crowned with darkness gathering behind like the illimitable resources of a dream. I tried to persuade him to leave the accursed den, and he wished—but —but—perhaps he *didn't* wish on the whole."

And to their later relations a touching letter of Carlyle's, in 1868, bears witness :—

"DEAR FITZGERALD,—Thanks for inquiring after me again. I am in my usual weak state of bodily health, not much worse, I imagine, and not even expecting to be better. I study to be solitary, in general ; to be silent, as the state that suits me best ; my thoughts then are infinitely sad indeed, but capable too of being solemn, mournfully beautiful, useful ; and as for ' happiness,' I have of that employment more or less befitting the years I have arrived at, and the long journey that cannot now be far off.

" Your letter has really entertained me : I could willingly accept twelve of that kind in the year—twelve, I say, or even fifty-two, if they could be content with an answer of *silent* thanks and friendly thoughts and remembrances ! But within the last three or four years my right hand has become captious, taken to shaking as you see, and all writing is a thing I require *compulsion* and close necessity to drive me into ! Why not call here when you come to town ? I again assure you that it would give me pleasure, and be a welcome and wholesome solace to me.—With many true wishes and regards, I am always, Dear F., sincerely yours,

"T. CARLYLE."

It is obvious that FitzGerald's later views of Carlyle, and even of his writing, were much modified by their friendship. In early days he had hated with a deep hatred the torrent of language, the mannerisms, the affectations, the " canvas waves " of Carlyle.

Thus he wrote to Bernard Barton of *The French Revolution* :—

" This state of head has not been improved by trying to get through a new book much in fashion—Carlyle's *French Revolution,*—written in a German style. An Englishman writes of French Revolutions in a German style. People say the Book is very deep : but it appears to me that the meaning *seems* deep from lying under mystical language. There is no repose, nor equable movement in it : all cut up into short sentences half reflective, half narrative ; so that one labours through it as vessels do through what is called a short sea—small, contrary going waves caused by shallows, and straits, and meeting tides, etc. I like to sail before the wind over the surface of an even-rolling eloquence like that of Bacon or the Opium Eater."

But as soon as Fitzgerald began to know him he also began to realise that Carlyle the writer was the same as Carlyle the man, and that what might have been called affectation in many writers was merely Carlyle's natural mode of expressing his thoughts. Still he could not tolerate the turgid, glowing, rugged rhetoric that came out like a series of explosions, though he maintained that there was "vital good" in all Carlyle wrote.

The thought of the philosopher sitting in his study, growling and fulminating about all things in heaven and earth, "scolding away at Darwin, the Turks, etc.," was always inexpressibly ludicrous to FitzGerald; and while he admired Carlyle's incredible energy and patience, with a kind of regretful wonder, seeing qualities displayed that were so unlike his own, he yet was offended by the rough indifference to the feelings of others—"a little Scotch indelicacy"—into which Carlyle was so often betrayed.

When in 1875, on the occasion of Carlyle's eightieth birthday, his admirers presented him with a commemorative gold medal, bearing Carlyle's effigy and an inscription, FitzGerald was considerably disconcerted. His dislike of anything resembling pose, of public recognition, came out very strongly ; he wrote :—

"And yet I think he might have declined the Honours of a Life of 'Heroism.' I have no doubt he would have played a Brave Man's Part if called on ; but, meanwhile, he has only sat pretty comfortably at Chelsea, scolding all the world for

not being Heroic, and not always very precise in telling them
how. He has, however, been so far heroic, as to be always
independent whether of Wealth, Rank, and Coteries of all
sorts : nay, apt to fly in the face of some who courted him.
I suppose he is changed, or subdued, at eighty : but up to
the last ten years he seemed to me just the same as when I
first knew him five-and-thirty years ago. What a Fortune he
might have made by showing himself about as a Lecturer, as
Thackeray and Dickens did ; I don't mean they did it for
Vanity : but to make money : and that to spend generously.
Carlyle did indeed lecture near forty years ago before he was
a Lion to be shown, and when he had but few Readers. . . .
He looked very handsome then, with his black hair, fine
Eyes, and a sort of Crucified Expression."

Carlyle himself kept a very warm corner in his
heart for FitzGerald. So much so indeed that that
sharp censor of all that was dilettante or inactive was
able actually to suppress all or nearly all contemptuous
comment on his friend.

Carlyle wrote of FitzGerald to Norton :—

"It is possible FitzGerald may have written to you ; but
whether or not I will send you his letter to myself, as a
slight emblem and memorial of the peaceable, affectionate,
and ultra modest man, and his innocent *far niente* life—and
the connexion (were there nothing more) of Omar, the
Mahometan Blackguard, and Oliver Cromwell, the English
Puritan !—discharging you completely, at the same time, from
ever returning me this letter, or taking any notice of it, except
a small silent one."

When the *Reminiscences* came out after Carlyle's
death, FitzGerald felt considerable indignation at
the brutality with which living persons, and near
relations of the living, were criticised. This indignation was, however, more directed against the editor
than against the writer ; and his admiration of Carlyle's
own strength and simplicity survived the shock.

When the Biography appeared, FitzGerald's feelings underwent an entire revulsion. His sense of indignation at the harshness displayed in the *Reminiscences* was swallowed up in admiration and love. He saw the nobleness of the man, his true tenderness of heart, the fiery trials through which he had passed, the faults of temperament with which he had so gallantly struggled. The book moved him deeply ; he wrote :—

" Yes, you must read Froude's *Carlyle* above all things, and tell me if you do not feel as I do about it. . . .

" But how is it that I did not know that Carlyle was so good, grand, and even loveable, till I read the Letters which Froude now edits ? I regret that I did not know what the Book tells us while Carlyle was still alive ; that I might have loved him as well as admired him. But Carlyle never spoke of himself in that way : I never heard him advert to his Works and his Fame, except one day he happened to mention ' About the time when Men began to talk of me.' "

It is an interesting friendship because so unequal. It shows that respect, and affection, and sincerity are the true levellers of all differences. Two men could hardly have been selected whose temperaments were not only so dissimilar, but to each of whom the faults of the other's intellect and character would have been naturally so repugnant. The gentle-hearted sceptic and the puritan prophet. Yet both had an eye for humanity and simplicity ; and upon these qualities their mutual regard was based.

Thackeray was at Trinity with FitzGerald, but his junior by two years. At Cambridge they were very close comrades. They were often in each other's rooms, and amused themselves with music and drawing ; they found infinite relish in criticising and caricaturing their friends and acquaintances, in imitating the peculiarities of singers, and maintaining the

brisk freemasonry of gifted and high-spirited youth.
Thackeray was "Will" to FitzGerald. FitzGerald by
turns Ned, Neddibus, Neddikins, Yedward, old Fitz,
or "dear *vieux*" to Thackeray. Thackeray was idle at
Cambridge. "I find reading a hard, hard matter," he
wrote to his mother; and he encouraged FitzGerald to
find it hard too. But their comradeship did not last
very long, though they met in town not infrequently,
and even visited Paris together. There was a radical
difference between the two men. Thackeray had a
full-blooded love of life and living, and an inveterate
sociability of disposition. FitzGerald had far less
vitality and animal spirits, and found the kind of life
in which Thackeray revelled a decided strain. Both
had moods of melancholy; but in Thackeray it was
rather the reaction from the excitement of eager
living, while in FitzGerald it was a melancholy of
temperament which lay deeper in his nature. We see
FitzGerald, as the years went on, turning more and
more to solitude and seclusion, country rambles alone
or with a single companion, loving the quiet sights
and sounds of nature, and instinctively avoiding the
strain of society and talk. Thackeray, on the other
hand, was made for cities and the stir of vivid and
vigorous life. FitzGerald wrote of him in 1845 :—

"In the mean while old Thackeray laughs at all this; and
goes on in his own way; writing hard for half-a-dozen
Reviews and Newrpapers all the morning; dining, drinking,
and talking of a night; managing to preserve a fresh colour
and perpetual flow of spirits under a wear-and-tear of thinking and feeding that would have knocked up any other man
I know two years ago, at least. . . ."

As the years went on, Thackeray's mundane successes made FitzGerald more and more shy of him,
and possibly even unconsciously a little jealous. Fitz-

Gerald appears to have been almost appalled at
Thackeray's zest and power of enjoyment; he was
bewildered at the knowledge of the world and human
weaknesses which Thackeray showed. And, moreover,
though Thackeray had a vein of deep and wholesome
tenderness in his nature, there was also a certain
cynicism, which to FitzGerald was unpalatable.
Thackeray's heroes and heroines enjoy the kingdoms
of the world and the glory of them; and the quiet,
domestic tenderness of life, the simple pleasures of the
family and the home, are rather as gentle interludes
in the fuller and more eager music of the glittering
world. It is all there, the softer and serener atmo-
sphere; but with Thackeray home-life is rather the
quiet interval, the haven into which, after the stress
of the voyage, the rattle of the ropes, the leaping of
the high seas, men return in weariness or disappoint-
ment. Thackeray's heroes are like Tennyson's Ulysses
—the world is set in their hearts, and they drink
delight of battle with their peers.

All this was foreign to FitzGerald; the current of
life was for him the quiet, monotonous movement of
leisure and simple joys. The life of cities he regarded
rather as a tonic, which should brace his spirit; and
should send him back with a keener zest to his garden
and his study, and the talk of simple persons in the
country stillness.

Life in London seemed to FitzGerald to have somehow taken off the bloom from the generous and high-
spirited boy he had known. But what the two felt, *imo
sub pectore*, for each other, comes out in a most touching
letter written by Thackeray to FitzGerald on the eve
of his departure for a lecturing tour in America in
1852, in which Thackeray says that if anything were
to happen to him, "I should like my daughters to

remember that you are the best and oldest friend their Father ever had, and that you would act as such: as my literary executor and so forth." He continues:—

"Does not this sound gloomily? Well: who knows what Fate is in store: and I feel not at all downcast, but very grave and solemn just at the brink of a great voyage . . . the great comfort I have in thinking about my dear old boy is that recollection of our youth when we loved each other as I now do while I write Farewell."

Yet they gradually drifted apart. Thackeray died on 24th December 1863, a worn-out man. "I have taken too many crops out of my brain," he had said, not long before. A fortnight later FitzGerald wrote to Samuel Laurence the painter:—

"Frederic Tennyson sent me a Photograph of W. M. T., old, white, massive, and melancholy, sitting in his Library.

"I am surprized almost to find how much I am thinking of him: so little as I had seen him for the last ten years; not once for the last five. I had been told—by you, for one—that he was spoiled. I am glad, therefore, that I have scarce seen him since he was 'old Thackeray.' I keep reading his *Newcomes* of nights, and, as it were, hear him saying so much in it; and it seems to me as if he might be coming up my Stairs, and about to come (singing) into my Room, as in old Charlotte Street, etc., thirty years ago."

The thought of his lost friend, in tender retrospect, was very often with him; the very echo of his footstep and the sound of his voice dwelt with him.

And he had, too, moods in which he admired Thackeray's work, though he did not feel it really congenial to him. "Fielding's seem to me coarse work in comparison," he wrote.

It is clear that Thackeray's own regard for FitzGerald never wavered. The difference between them was temperamental: and it was inevitable that FitzGerald

should become conscious of the dissimilarity, though
there was no reason why Thackeray should.   It may
be remembered that, in the later days of his writing,
Thackeray professed himself unable to write in his
own study ; he found it necessary to go to the Club or
even to an hotel to stimulate his brain by the sight and
scent, so to speak, of life.   Apart from the movement
and stir of human beings, he was overmastered by
depression and dreariness.   Such a taste would not be
only unintelligible but positively repellent to Fitz-
Gerald.   And it was this deep-seated divergence of
temperament that made companionship impossible ;
though there is no failure of love or even loyalty to
record.

James Spedding was probably the most revered and
admired, and perhaps the most deeply, if not the most
warmly loved of all FitzGerald's friends.   From the
earliest Spedding had a great reputation for *mitis
sapientia*.   " He was the Pope among us young men,"
said Tennyson, " the wisest man I knew."   With more
levity FitzGerald and Thackeray used to make merry
over Spedding's high, dome-shaped forehead, prematurely bald.

" That portrait of Spedding, for instance, which Laurence
has given me : not swords, nor cannon, nor all the Bulls of
Bashan butting at it, could, I feel sure, discompose that venerable forehead.   No wonder that no hair can grow at such an
altitude : no wonder his view of Bacon's virtue is so rarefied
that the common consciences of men cannot endure it.
Thackeray and I occasionally amuse ourselves with the idea
of Spedding's forehead : we find it somehow or other in all
things, just peering out of all things : you see it in a mile-
stone, Thackeray says.   He also draws the forehead rising
with a sober light over Mont Blanc, and reflected in the lake
of Geneva.   We have great laughing over this.   The fore-

head is at present in Pembrokeshire, I believe : or Glamor-
ganshire : or Monmouthshire : it is hard to say which.   It
has gone to spend its Christmas there."

Spedding was the son of a Cumberland squire.   After
leaving Cambridge he went to the bar and devoted himself eventually to the editing of Bacon's works ; a task
which lasted over thirty years.   After holding one or
two temporary appointments, Spedding was offered,
in 1847, the Permanent Under-Secretaryship for the
Colonies, on the retirement of Sir James Stephen, who
wrote of Spedding that he was "gentle, luminous, and
in his own quiet way energetic."   He would not, however, desert Bacon.   Spedding was a man of wonderfully calm, well-balanced, and thoughtful temperament,
and was the trusted friend and adviser of many
families.   "He always seemed to regard himself," said
Sir Leslie Stephen, "from the outside, as a good-
natured man might regard a friend whose foibles
amuse him, but who is at bottom not a bad fellow."
He was averse to recognition ; he refused an honorary
degree, and, on Charles Kingsley's resignation, the
Professorship of Modern History at Cambridge, with
humorous and lucid explanations of his own inadequacy.
FitzGerald's love and admiration for Spedding never
varied ; though it is not uncharacteristic that he
could write of him, after fifty years of friendship, in
the terms of the following letter, and yet make no
attempt to see him :—

"My dear old Spedding, though I have not seen him these
twenty years and more—and probably should never see him
again—but he lives—his old Self—in my heart of hearts ;
and all I hear of him does but embellish the recollection of
him—if it could be embellished—for he is but the same that
he was from a Boy—all that is best in Heart and Head—a
man that would be incredible had one not known him."

F

A few days after this letter was written, Spedding was run over by a cab and carried to St. George's Hospital, where, on the 9th of March 1881, he died.

On the 13th of March FitzGerald wrote :—

"It seems almost wrong or unreasonable of me to be talking thus of myself and my little Doings, when not only Carlyle has departed from us, but one, not so illustrious in Genius, but certainly not less wise, my dear old Friend of sixty years, James Spedding : whose name you will know as connected with Lord Bacon. To re-edit his Works, which did not want any such re-edition, and to vindicate his Character, which could not be cleared, did this Spedding sacrifice forty years which he might well have given to accomplish much greater things ; Shakespeare, for one. But Spedding had no sort of ambition, and liked to be kept at one long work which he knew would not glorify himself. He was the wisest man I have known : not the less so for plenty of the Boy in him ; a great sense of Humour, a Socrates in Life and in Death, which he faced with all Serenity so long as Consciousness lasted."

And again, writing of him a few days later, he said :—

"Laurence had written me some account of his Visit to St. George's : all Patience : only somewhat wishful to be at home : somewhat weary with lying without Book, or even Watch, for company. What a Man ! as in Life so in Death, which, as Montaigne says, proves what is at the bottom of the Vessel. . . .

"He did not want to see me ; he wanted nothing, I think : but I was always thinking of him, and should have done till my own Life's end, I know."

Thus, in the region of friendship, as in all other sides of life, we see how early the glow of youth, of companionship, of joy deserted FitzGerald, and left him living in a tender, retrospective dream. Many men are content to let their youthful friendships fade

into oblivion, to allow propinquity and circumstance
to determine their choice of associates, or to concentrate their interests upon a closer family circle.
But FitzGerald was loyal and faithful to the old ties;
and his fidelity prevailed even over the clear-sighted
microscopic gaze which he brought to bear on character and life, and to which so much of his own
unhappiness was due.

CHAPTER V

It will be convenient here briefly to summarise the writings of FitzGerald, with the dates of their issue.

First comes the *Selection from the Poems and Letters of Bernard Barton*, with a Memoir by FitzGerald, published in 1849 by Hall, Virtue and Co.

Next comes the *Euphranor*, which was published by Pickering in 1851. *Polonius*, a collection of aphorisms, which has been already described, was published by Pickering in 1852. In 1853 came the *Six Dramas of Calderon*, published by Pickering. The second edition of *Euphranor*, much altered, appeared in 1855, published by J. W. Parker. In 1856 appeared *Salámán and Absál*, published by Parker, which was reprinted at Ipswich in 1871, though FitzGerald seems to have ignored the issue. In 1859 came the first edition of *Omar Khayyám*, published by Quaritch. In 1862 this was privately reprinted in India, with a few additional quatrains, and some illustrative matter. In 1865 two dramas from Calderon—*The Mighty Magician* and *Such Stuff as Dreams are made of*, printed by Childs, and intended for private distribution. In the same year 1865, the translation of the *Agamemnon* was privately printed. In 1868 appeared the second edition of the *Omar*, published by Quaritch. In 1871, as I have said, a few copies of a revised edition of *Salámán and Absál* were printed at Ipswich. In 1872 the third edition

of *Omar* was published by Quaritch.   In 1876 the
Agamemnon was published by Quaritch, who in 1879
published the fourth edition of the *Omar* together with
the *Salámán and Absál*.   In the same year the first
part of the *Readings in Crabbe* was privately printed
by Billing.   In 1880 the first part of the *Œdipus*, and
in 1881 the second part, were printed by Billing.
In 1882 a revised *Euphranor* was printed by the same
firm.   In 1882 the *Readings in Crabbe* was published by
Quaritch, and in 1883 the second part of the *Readings
in Crabbe* was published by Quaritch.

The above record clearly illustrates the desire in
FitzGerald's mind to print his works, together with his
shrinking from publication.   None of his publications,
except the *Six Dramas of Calderon*, bore his name, and
this only in order to avoid confusion with another
almost contemporary translation.   He preferred to
test the merits of a book by distributing a few copies
among his friends; and the record shows too, in the
constant revision and alteration that his work received, the extreme difficulty which he found in satis-
fying his instinct for perfection.   The result is that
the bibliography of his writings is a matter of great
complexity.

It is natural to regret the fact that FitzGerald did not
more often attempt to speak to the world with his own
direct, authentic utterance.   But a temperament both
melancholy and fastidious is never in want of reasons
for holding its peace.   Very early in life his impulse
towards creative and original work died away.   Thus
he wrote to Bernard Barton in 1842 :—

" As to my doing anything else in that way, I know that I
could write volume after volume as well as others of the mob
of gentlemen who write with ease : but I think unless a man
can do better, he had best not do at all ; I have not the

strong inward call, nor cruel-sweet pangs of parturition, that prove the birth of anything bigger than a mouse."

And again to the same :—

" I am a man of taste, of whom there are hundreds born every year : only that less easy circumstances than mine at present are compel them to one calling : that calling perhaps a mechanical one, which overlies all their other, and naturally perhaps more energetic impulses. As to an occasional copy of verses, there are few men who have leisure to read, and are possessed of any music in their souls, who are not capable of versifying on some ten or twelve occasions during their natural lives : at a proper conjunction of the stars. There is no harm in taking advantage of such occasions."

The truth is that FitzGerald's mind was deficient in the imaginative quality. He had a strong spectatorial interest in life, a kind of dark yet tender philosophy, which gave him his one great opportunity : but even there he had, like Teucer, to shoot his arrows behind the shield of Ajax. He had, of course, an extra-ordinary delicacy of perception ; but on the critical side.

His strength lay in his power of expressing, with a sort of careful artlessness, elusive thoughts, rather than in strength or subtlety of invention. His timid, fastidious imagination shrank from the strain of con-structing, originating, creating. The *Euphranor*, which will be considered later in detail, is the only experiment that he made in the direction of fiction, and there is no dramatic grasp in it, no firm delineation of character ; one feels that he is moving puppets to and fro, and the voice of the showman is speaking all the time. He had, too, a certain feminine irritability, a peevish fastidiousness which would have dogged his steps if he had embarked upon a larger subject ; he would never have been satisfied with his work ; he would have fretted over it, and abandoned it in despair.

He was deficient, too, in the patience requisite for
carrying work through.   "To correct is *the* Bore," he
wrote to Cowell.   Yet the bulky volumes of extracts
and selections and abridgements, which remain in Mr.
Aldis Wright's possession, such as the collection
whimsically named *Half-Hours with the Worst Authors*,
testify to a certain laboriousness, an acquisitiveness, a
species of diligence which cannot be gainsaid.   One
may wonder, too, that so desultory a student contrived
to translate so much as FitzGerald did; but his mind
was in a sense active; he could not be unoccupied, and
yet had not the vigour necessary for original work.
To such a man it is a comfort to have work which
demands no expenditure of vital force, which may be
taken up and laid down at will, and where the original
supplies the literary impulse.

But what is perhaps at the root of the matter is that
FitzGerald always subordinated Art to Life. He had little
of the fierce, imperative, creative impulse.   Art seemed
to him not a thing apart, but an accessory of life; and
therefore a single touch of nature was to FitzGerald a
higher thing than the highest achievement of art.

Thus he had a great tenderness for worthless little
books, if they only revealed some gentle and delicate
trait of character, some small piece of wistful individuality.   A great conception, a broad and vigorous
motive, often bewildered and stupefied him.   His idea
of the paradise of art was as of a place where you
could wander quietly about picking a flower here
and there, catching a little effect, watching a pretty
grouping of trees and water, the sunlight on a grassy
bank or a gable-end.   He lived and thought in a series
of glimpses and vistas, but the plan of the place, its
avenues and terraces, was unregarded by him.   And
thus there was a want of centrality, of combination,

of breadth, about his mind. Art was to him not an
impassioned quest, but a leisurely wandering in search
of charm, of colour, of subtle impressions. Probably
FitzGerald never truly estimated his own temperament.
He was perhaps misled by his gentle ecstasies into
thinking that an effort was all that was needed; and
perhaps, too, he liked to fancy that what was in reality
a deep-seated languor of will, was a philosophical
unworldliness, an indifference to rewards and crowns.
He nourished no illusions about his past; but he had
hopes of future performance, though no care for fame;
and it was only as day after day sank like ripples into
the pool behind him, that he became aware that the
necessary effort would probably not be made.

No doubt too, to a man of FitzGerald's disposition,
the absolute indifference shown by the world at large
to his writings deprived him of the last touch of
stimulus. What was still more disheartening, even his
friends took comparatively little interest in his doings.
Dean Merivale said in 1877 that he had " never thought
FitzGerald was guilty of verse."

Perhaps a great and incontestable success early in
life might have made a difference to him; but even so
he would have been easily cast down by criticism and
depreciation. He had not the physical vigour to enjoy
success, the full-blooded energy that makes a man
desire to be felt, to create a stir, to wield an influence,
to be a personage. He would probably have found
that his success gave him only a temporary elation,
and that the draught had something heady and
poisonous about it. He would have taken no
pleasure in unintelligent appreciation, in the numeri-
cal increase of circulation which shows at all events
that a man's work is accepted by the deferential
readers who follow authority humbly.

It is then not to be wondered at, that with Fitz-Gerald's earnest avoidance of publicity, his shrinking from criticism, such neglect should have been the result. But it served only to increase his natural diffidence and to make him despair of ever realising the ambitious dreams which he had once nourished in the careless days of youth, before he had felt the cold shadow of the world, before he had learned that he was to die.

Of FitzGerald's writings, I propose to deal first with his translations from the Oriental poets, whom he began to read with Cowell, probably in 1853. Jámí's *Salámán and Absál* appeared first, being published in 1856. In the same year he began to read Attar's *Bird Parliament*, and was working in his leisurely way at *Omar Khayyám*, reading, enjoying and adapting.

Jámí's *Salámán and Absál* is an allegory over which FitzGerald spent much time and care ; it is idle to speculate why, when the work is compared with *Omar*, the achievement appears to be so slight. Yet so it is. The truth is, I conceive, that FitzGerald put so little of himself into the poem, but was content to ride, as it were, in Jámí's chariot.

The poem is prefaced by an interesting, though some-what vague, letter to Cowell, discussing the difficulties of dealing with so diffuse a poet as Jámí, and explaining that in his version he has sacrificed much of the Oriental imagery.

But there is a touching autobiographical passage in the letter which may be quoted. He writes :—

"In studying the Original, you know, one gets contentedly carried over barren Ground in a new Land of Language—excited by chasing any new Game that will but show Sport ; the most worthless to win asking perhaps all the sharper

Energy to pursue, and so far giving all the more Satisfaction when run down. Especially, cheered on as I was by such a Huntsman as poor Dog of a Persian Scholar never hunted with before; and moreover—but that was rather in the Spanish Sierras—by the Presence of a Lady in the Field, silently brightening about us like Aurora's Self, or chiming in with musical Encouragement that all we started and ran down must be Royal Game.

"Oh, happy days! When shall we Three meet again—when dip in that returning Tide of Time and Circumstance! In those Meadows far from the World, it seemed, as Salámán's Island—before an iron Railway broke the Heart of the Happy Valley whose Gossip was the Mill-wheel, and Visitors the Summer Airs that momentarily ruffled the Sleepy Stream that turned it as they chased one another over to lose themselves in whispers in the Copse beyond. Or returning—I suppose you remember whose Lines they are—

> " ' When Winter Skies were tinged with Crimson still
>   Where Thornbush nestles on the quiet hill,
>   And the live Amber round the setting Sun,
>   Lighting the Labourer home whose Work is done,
>   Burn'd like a Golden Angel-ground above
>   The solitary Home of Peace and Love.' [1]

"At such an hour drawing home together for a fireside Night of it with Æschylus or Calderon in the Cottage, whose walls, modest almost as those of the Poor who clustered—and with good reason—round, make to my Eyes the Towered Crown of Oxford hanging in the Horizon, and with all Honour won, but a dingy Vapour in Comparison. And now, should they beckon from the terrible Ganges, and this little Book, begun as a happy Record of past, and pledge perhaps of future, Fellowship in Study, darken already with the shadow of everlasting Farewell!"

There is a short note on the original metre of the poem; and a little biographical sketch of Jámí, slight

---

[1] Written by Mrs. Cowell, and altered (for the better) by FitzGerald. The original is given in Cowell's *Life*, p. 307. Thornbush is the name of a farm above Bramford.

enough, as must needs be the case with the legend of one of whom comparatively little is known, but over which FitzGerald lingers tenderly, strewing roses by the way.

Jámí was born early in the fifteenth century of the Christian era ; he was a precocious and learned child ; he went to   great school at Samarcand, but was recalled to Herat by a dream, and there devoted himself to the religious life, joining the mystical Súfí sect, withdrawing into profound solitude, and becoming a silent, visionary man, absorbed in contemplation. But he could not resist the impulse of poetry. "A thousand times," he says, "I have repented of such Employment; but I could no more shirk it than one can shirk what the Pen of Fate has written on his Forehead." "As Poet I have resounded through the world ; Heaven filled itself with my Song. . . . The Kings of India and Rúm greet me by Letter; the Lords of Irák and Tabríz load me with gifts." After a pilgrimage to Mecca, with some sharp adventures intermingled, he returned to Herat ; died at a great age, and was buried with much pomp and circumstance. He wrote innumerable volumes of grammar, poetry, and theology. *Salámán and Absál* was the last product of his old age, the mature vintage of his powers.

It is an allegory in which, as FitzGerald says, the poet "symbolised an esoteric doctrine which he dared not—and probably could not—more intelligibly reveal." Its obscurity is not diminished by the fact that it is broken by many apparently irrelevant episodes, several of them of a humorous character.

FitzGerald translated the main poem into blank verse and the episodes into a brisk, unrhymed Trochaic metre, with Paroemiac pauses.

Perhaps the most effective passage occurs in the
introductory invocation :—

" And yet, how long, O Jámí, stringing Verse,
  Pearl after pearl, on that old Harp of thine ?
Year after year attuning some new Song,
  The breath of some old Story ? Life is gone,
And that last song is not the last ; my Soul
  Is spent—and still a Story to be told !
And I, whose back is crooked as the Harp
  I still keep tuning through the Night till Day !
That harp untuned by Time—the harper's hand
  Shaking with Age—how shall the harper's hand
Repair its cunning, and the sweet old harp
  Be modulated as of old ? Methinks
'Twere time to break and cast it in the fire ;
  The vain old harp, that breathing from its strings
No music more to charm the ears of men,
  May, from its scented ashes, as it burns,
Breathe resignation to the Harper's soul,
  Now that his body looks to dissolution.

   ·   ·   ·   ·   ·   ·   ·   ·

Pain sits with me sitting behind my knees,
  From which I hardly rise unhelpt of hand ;
I bow down to my root, and like a Child
  Yearn, as is likely, to my Mother Earth,
Upon whose bosom I shall cease to weep,
  And on my Mother's bosom fall asleep."

The story is thus—the Shah of Yúnan prays for a
son ; and a divinely gifted child, Salámán, of extraordinary beauty, strength, and wit, is sent him. The
child is nursed by a young foster-mother Absál. As
he grows to manhood, Salámán learns to love her, and
sinks into idle dalliance. He is rebuked by the Shah
and by a Sage, and bidden to live more manfully. He
determines to fly with Absál, sets forth for the desert,
and reaches a wide sea where he embarks on a magic

skiff, which bears the pair to an isle of Paradise; there
for a while they dwell, till, struck by contrition, he
returns, and, torn between duty and passion, resolves
to die with Absál. They fling themselves together
into a pyre, but though Absál perishes, Salámán is
preserved by magical arts.

In the second part Salámán slowly climbs out of his
despair, learns wisdom, and is crowned King. There
follows a long, mystical interpretation of the parable,
which is little more than the old thought of the
Conquest of Self, nursed by Pleasure, wrought out by
suffering.

The finest passage is probably the description of the
great sea :—

> " Six days Salámán on the Camel rode,
> And then the hissing arrows of reproof
> Were fallen far behind ; and on the Seventh
> He halted on the Seashore ; on the shore
> Of a great Sea that reaching like a floor
> Of rolling firmament below the Sky's
> From Káf to Káf, to Gau and Máhí [1] down
> Descended, and its Stars were living eyes.
> The Face of it was as it were a range
> Of moving Mountains ; or a countless host
> Of Camels trooping tumultuously up,
> Host over host, and foaming at the lip.
> Within, innumerable glittering things
> Sharp as cut Jewels, to the sharpest eye
> Scarce visible, hither and thither slipping,
> As silver scissors slice a blue brocade."

There is a certain Oriental splendour about this ;
but it is loosely put together, and there are obvious
faults both of metre and language.

The whole translation, it must be confessed, is a
languid performance. The figure of FitzGerald seems

[1] The mystical boundaries and bases of the world.

to move and pace as it were uneasily, embarrassed and encumbered by the rich and pictorial draperies. One feels that he was following the original too closely, and had not the courage boldly to discard the Eastern imagery, as he did in *Omar*, where he selected enough to give his version an Oriental colouring while he escaped from the weight of the unfamiliar and overloaded texture. He was aware, indeed, that he had not wholly succeeded with *Salámán*; he wrote to Norton :—

" Omar remains as he was ; Jámí (Salámán) is cut down to two-thirds of his former proportion, and very much improved, I think. It is still in a wrong key : Verse of Miltonic strain, unlike the simple Eastern ; I remember trying that at first, but could not succeed. So there is little but the Allegory itself (not a bad one), and now condensed into a very fair Bird's Eye view ; quite enough for any Allegory, I think. . . ."

The *Salámán and Absál* is indeed interesting only in the light of *Omar*, as revealing the process whereby rich results were attained, though it is hard to repress a sense of wonder that the uncertain hand which penned the *Salámán* can have worked in the same material with such firm and easy strokes as were employed in the *Omar*.

The interest, then, is almost purely critical, the interest of an early essay in an art in which the author afterwards attained so splendid a mastery.

The *Bird Parliament*, by Attar, attracted FitzGerald's attention about 1856. In 1857 an edition of the text was published by Garcin de Tassy, who had previously analysed the poem. FitzGerald began to study the book carefully, and wrote to Cowell in India that the apologues were shaping themselves into verse. In 1862 he had finished a verse-translation which he intended at one time to publish in the *Journal of the Bengal Asiatic Society*; but he became aware that it

was too free a version to be given in the pages of a
scientific publication. The plot is as follows :—

The birds assemble to choose a king; and recite
their several claims to sovereignty. The Tajidar
(Crown-wearer), or Persian Lapwing, acts as a kind
of Moderator. The Tajidar has travelled the Road
of faith, and has attained to the knowledge of
the presence of God; after the birds have finished
their statements, the Tajidar expounds the mysteries
of faith and attainment. His words inspire the faithful
birds with enthusiasm. The Tajidar is crowned King,
and after a long, mystical discourse on the nature
of the search for truth, a chosen band sets off on
Pilgrimage, the more mundane and secular of the
birds retiring to their ordinary occupations. Some
thirty, under the guidance of the Tajidar, attain to
the vision of God. Thus it may be said that the plot
is somewhat analogous to that of *The Holy Grail.*

It is a carefully wrought poem, extending to many
hundred lines; but it must be confessed that the
Oriental flavour is too strong; the discursiveness, the
lack of definite design, the excess of ornament are
both irritating and unsatisfying. The narrative is
broken by the intrusion of many little fables and
allegories ; this device, somewhat resembling the
inclusion of box within box, lacquered and gilded, is
highly characteristic of the tangential and desultory
Oriental mind, but to a Western reader, it tends
merely to confuse the structure of the poem.

Much has been said and written about FitzGerald's
Omar Khayyám; it has received from its admirers the
sort of treatment, the poking and pushing, conceded to
prize animals at shows; it has been made the subject
of microscopical investigation ; the alterations made by

FitzGerald himself in the various editions have afforded
a rich field for textual comparison and criticism. Yet
the origin of the poem can be very simply stated.
FitzGerald happened to light upon an ancient poet,
through whose writings, in spite of much tedious
iteration and dreary moralising, much sensual imagery
and commonplace Epicureanism, ran a vein of thought
strangely familiar to his own temperament. Omar
was a sentimentalist, and a lover of beauty, both
human and natural; so was FitzGerald. Omar tended
to linger over golden memories of the past, and was
acutely alive to the pathos of sweet things that have an
ending; and such was FitzGerald. Omar was penetrated with a certain dark philosophy, the philosophy
of the human spirit at bay, when all refuge has failed;
and this was the case with FitzGerald.

The result was that out of the ore which was
afforded him, FitzGerald, by this time a practised
craftsman without a subject, was enabled to chase and
chisel his delicate stanzas, like little dainty vessels of
pure gold. He brought to the task a rich and stately
vocabulary, and a style adapted to solemn and somewhat rhetorical musings of a philosophical kind. Fitz-
Gerald's love of slow-moving verse adorned by beautiful
touches of natural observation and of pathetic present-
ment stood him in good stead. The result was that a
man of high literary taste found for once a subject
precisely adapted to his best faculty; a subject, the
strength of which was his own strength, and the
limitations of which were his own limitations.

Moreover, the poem was fortunate both in the time
and manner of its appearance; there was a wave of
pessimism astir in the world, the pessimism of an age
that dares not live without pleasure, in whose mouth
simplicity is a synonym for dulness, tortured alike by

its desires and by the satiety of their satisfaction, and overshadowed by the inherited conscience which it contemns but cannot disregard.

Further, it was fortunate in the manner of its appearance. If FitzGerald had presented the world with an original poem of dreary scepticism and desperate philosophy, he would have found but few hearers. But the sad and wasted form of his philosophy came slowly forwards, dimly smiling, draped in this rich Oriental fabric, and with all the added mystery of venerable antiquity. It heightened the charm to readers, living in a season of outworn faith and restless dissatisfaction, to find that eight hundred years before, far across the centuries, in the dim and remote East, the same problems had pressed sadly on the mind of an ancient and accomplished sage. They did not realise to what an extent FitzGerald had concentrated the scattered rays into his burning-glass; nor how much of the poignant sadness, the rich beauty of the thought had been overlaid upon the barer texture of the original writer by the far more sensitive and perceptive mind of the translator. It was as though FitzGerald had found some strict and solemn melody of a bygone age, and enriched it with new and honeyed harmonies, added melancholy cadences and sweet interludes of sorrow. He always tended, as Cowell wrote to Mr. Aldis Wright, "to put in some touch of his own large hand . . . beyond the author's outline."

There is little that need be said, little indeed that can be said, about the style which FitzGerald adopted for his *Omar*. It is not due to any special poetical tradition; the poem is written in a grave, resonant English of a stately kind, often with a certain Latinity of phrase, and yet never really avoiding a homely directness both of diction and statement. His aim

G

appears to have been to produce melodious, lucid, and epigrammatic stanzas, which should as far as possible follow the general lines of the original thought; but at the same time he did not hesitate to discard and suppress anything that interfered with his own conception of structure; no doubt the exigencies of rhyme to a certain extent influenced the line of his thought, because the triple rhyme which he employed is bound to impose fetters on the fancy; but he seems to have given no hint as to how he worked; the wonder rather is that anything which is of the nature of a paraphrase should succeed in achieving so profound an originality.

I do not propose, in the following pages, to treat the poem from the Orientalist point of view; it is a deeply interesting task, but demands a fulness and minuteness of treatment which puts it quite outside the scope of this biography; it has, moreover, been exhaustively done; and after all, it is the expression and spirit of the poem in English, and not its fidelity to or divergence from its Oriental original, which gives FitzGerald his position in the world of letters.

A careful study of FitzGerald's letters to Cowell in 1857, while the *Omar* was in process of construction, has revealed to me both how desultory his method was, and also how difficult he found the elucidation of the meaning. These letters have never been published —indeed they are too technical for publication—but have been shown me by Mr. Aldis Wright. FitzGerald seems to be constantly uncertain whether he had arrived at the true meaning of a passage: "I am not always quite certain of always getting the right sow by the ear," he writes at the conclusion of a long string of questions. The letters are written more like diaries; and he added to his queries day by day, as he made progress with the work.

The story of FitzGerald's acquaintance with the original book is interesting enough. His friend Cowell, who introduced him to the study of Oriental poetry, had found in the Bodleian, in the Ouseley collection, a rare manuscript, written on yellow paper "with purple-black ink profusely powdered with gold." Before leaving England for India, he made a transcript of this for FitzGerald, who carried it about with him, brooded over it, and worked slowly and leisurely at the task of adaptation.

Thus he wrote to Cowell:—

"When in Bedfordshire I put away almost all Books except *Omar Khayyám*! which I could not help looking over in a Paddock covered with Buttercups and brushed by a delicious Breeze, while a dainty racing Filly of W. Browne's came startling up to wonder and snuff about me. 'Tempus est quo Orientis Aura mundus renovatur, Quo de fonte pluviali dulcis Imber reseratur; *Musi-manus* undecumque ramos insuper splendescit; Jesu-spiritusque Salutaris terram pervagatur.'[1] Which is to be read as Monkish Latin, like 'Dies Irae,' etc., retaining the Italian value of the Vowels, not the Classical. You will think me a perfectly Aristophanic Old Man when I tell you how many of Omar I could not help running into such bad Latin. I should not confide such follies but to you who won't think them so, and who will be pleased at least with my still harping on our old Studies. You would be sorry, too, to think that Omar breathes a sort of Consolation to me. Poor Fellow; I think of him, and Oliver Basselin, and Anacreon; lighter Shadows among the Shades, perhaps, over which Lucretius presides so grimly."

In 1857 Cowell sent FitzGerald a further instalment of Omar literature, namely, a copy of a Calcutta manuscript, and a rare volume, which had been edited from that manuscript, and printed in 1836.

[1] A rendering, somewhat loose, of the stanza " Now the New Year," etc.

The writer of this book was one Omar Khayyám, who was living about the time of the Norman Conquest. He died probably in 1123. The legend goes that he and two fellow-pupils when boys at school took a vow that if any of them rose to eminence they would share their good fortune with the others. One of them became Vizier to the Sultan Alp-Arslán, the son of the Tartar, Toghrul Beg, founder of the Seljukian Dynasty, which finally roused Europe into the Crusades. The Vizier seeking out, or being sought out by, his old friends, gave to one, with a truly Oriental instinct for what would now be called jobbery, a place under Government, and to Omar, who was a man of scholarly tastes, a mathematician and an astronomer, a large pension. Omar was not a mere dilettante. He composed mathematical, metaphysical and scientific treatises. He was one of a Board who reformed the Calendar, a fact which he mentions in his poems. Omar appears to have been a man of self-contained and unsociable temperament, disinclined to labour, and given, at all events in later life, to gross self-indulgence. The recorded incidents of his life are but few, and much that is legendary is undoubtedly intertwined with them; but there is one which is so entirely in the spirit of FitzGerald that it must be repeated. Walking in a garden with a favourite pupil, he said one day, "My tomb shall be in a spot where the North wind may scatter roses over it." Many years after, when the young man visited the tomb of Omar at Nishapur, he found that the rose-trees of a neighbouring garden stretched their boughs over the wall, and strewed the tomb with "wreck of white and red."

The Bodleian MS. of the Rubáiyát or Quatrains, contains 158 stanzas, though many more are attributed

to him. They are not continuous as a rule, though
in some cases an episode runs through a number of
them. They are rather to be called epigrams, each
dealing, like a compressed sonnet, with some single
thought—with love and wine, beauty and charm,
life and death, and what lies beyond. But Fitz-
Gerald by selection and arrangement made a certain
progression or series out of them, tracing in vague
outline a soul's history.

FitzGerald wrote of the Rubáiyát that they "are
independent stanzas, consisting each of four lines of
equal, though varied, Prosody; sometimes *all* rhyming,
but oftener (as here imitated) the third line a blank.
Somewhat as in the Greek Alcaic, where the penulti-
mate line seems to lift and suspend the Wave that falls
over in the last. As usual with such kind of Oriental
Verse, the Rubáiyát follow one another according to
Alphabetic Rhyme—a strange succession of Grave and
Gay."

It seems that about half of FitzGerald's stanzas are
adaptations of single quatrains; about half are adapted
out of two or more quatrains; four show traces of
thoughts taken from other poets, Attar and Hafiz;
two are from quatrains of doubtful authority; and
three appear to have no original model; there are a few
others which similarly appear to be purely the work of
FitzGerald; but the fact that he discarded them in
later editions tends to prove that he was anxious to
preserve the idea of translation. Fitzgerald's principle
of interpolating lines from other stanzas is illustrated
by what he wrote to Cowell:—

"I think you might string together the stray good Lines
from some of the otherwise worthless Odes—empty Bottles!—
in a very good fashion which I will tell you about when we
meet."

One other point deserves to be mentioned. Fitz-
Gerald was for ever fretting over the quatrains and
retouching them; no less than four editions appeared
in his lifetime, containing many variations; and it is
clear that the more he altered, the more he tended to
diverge from the original thought. We may take two
or three typical instances of the process of alteration
which took place in the various editions of the poem.

Stanza i. originally stood :—

> "Awake! for Morning in the Bowl of Night
> Has flung the Stone that puts the Stars to Flight :
>   And lo! the Hunter of the East has caught
> The Sultán's Turret in a Noose of Light."

In the second edition this was altered to :—

> "Wake! for the Sun behind yon Eastern height
> Has chased the Session of the Stars from Night :
>   And, to the field of Heav'n ascending, strikes
> The Sultán's Turret with a Shaft of Light."

In the third edition (first draft) the first couplet of
the quatrain ran :—

> "Wake! for the Sun before him into Night
> A Signal flung that put the Stars to flight" :

In the fourth edition we read :—

> "Wake! for the Sun who scatter'd into flight
> The Stars before him from the Field of Night,
>   Drives Night along with them from Heav'n, and
>   strikes
> The Sultán's Turret with a Shaft of Light."

The original quatrain, literally translated by Mr.
Heron-Allen, runs :—

> "The Sun casts the noose of morning upon the roofs ;
> Kai Khosru [1] of the day, he throws a stone into the Bowl :

---

[1] This expression, which is merely the name of an ancient
Persian king, Chosroes I., is practically equivalent to
"sovereign Lord and Master."

> Drink wine ! for the Herald of the Dawn, rising up
> Hurls into the days the cry of 'Drink ye !'"

It will be seen by comparing these versions how the stanza travelled gradually further and further away from the imagery of the original; it may be questioned whether the first version is not the most beautiful; and it is certainly an imperfection in the latest version that the rhyme *Night* is repeated early in the third line, while the assonance of the vowel-sound of "strikes" hardly provides a strong enough contrast, considering that the relief given to the ear by the unrhymed ending of the third line is thus partially sacrificed.

Stanza x. of the first edition originally ran:—

> " With me along some strip of Herbage strown
> That just divides the desert from the sown
> Where name of Slave and Sultán scarce is known
> And pity Sultán Máhmúd on his throne."

An awkward and monotonous stanza.

In the second and later editions the quatrain runs:—

> " With me along *the* strip of Herbage strown
> That just divides the desert from the sown,
>   Where name of Slave and Sultán is forgot,
> And Peace to Máhmúd on his golden Throne !"

This stanza appears to have no original in the Persian, but to have been evolved out of FitzGerald's own mind, except that Omar sometimes speaks of the edge of the tilled country, "the green bank of a field" on which he loved to rest.

But the alterations are subtle and delicate; the change from "some" to "the" lightens the weight of the first line; the removal of the rhyme at the end of the third line gives relief; and few will doubt that the

wish that the Sultan may enjoy peace is more in
keeping with the contented mood than to think of him
with pity.　He is taken in, so to speak, into the inner
circle of sunshine which for an hour may lie upon the
sorrowing earth.

In the original edition, stanza xxxiii. ran :—

> " Then to the rolling Heav'n itself I cried,
> 　Asking ' What Lamp had Destiny to guide
> 　　Her little Children, stumbling in the Dark ?'
> 　And—'A blind Understanding !' Heav'n replied."

In the second edition, this stanza is swept away, and
the noble lines are substituted :—

> ' Earth could not answer, nor the Seas that mourn
> 　In flowing Purple, of their Lord forlorn ;
> 　　Nor Heaven, with those eternal signs reveal'd
> 　And hidden by the sleeve of Night and Morn."

In the third edition the third line becomes :—

> "Nor rolling Heaven, with all his signs reveal'd " ;

which is finally retained.[1]

There appears to be no original at all which suggested the first version ; and though the third line,
" Her little Children, stumbling in the dark," has a
pathos of simplicity, the quatrain is not wholly satisfactory, and the fourth line is unmetrical.　But the
sonorous stanza as it finally appears, based upon so
slender a hint, is not only noble in itself, but is penetrated by a true Oriental symbolism.

Again, in the original edition there stood a stanza
(No. xlv.) which seems to have had no parallel in the
text :—

---

[1] The original of this stanza is not to be found in Omar at
all, but in the poems of Attar.

> " But leave the Wise to wrangle, and with me
>   The Quarrel of the Universe let be ;
>   And, in some corner of the Hubbub coucht
>   Make Game of that which makes as much of Thee."

It may be questioned why this stanza has disappeared ; possibly it was because there was no original quatrain corresponding to it ; but I would incline to think that FitzGerald felt that the suggestion of mockery was a false note, and that mystery and wonder, and the pathos of short-lived beauty and happiness were rather the essence of his poem.

We may now consider in detail what are unquestionably the noblest stanzas of the poem.

In the first edition stanzas lvii. and lviii. ran as follows :—

> " Oh Thou, who didst with Pitfall and with Gin
>   Beset the road I was to wander in,
>   Thou wilt not with Predestination round
>   Enmesh me, and impute my fall to Sin.

> Oh Thou, who Man of baser Earth didst make,
>   And who with Eden didst devise the Snake :
>   For all the Sin wherewith the Face of Man
>   Is blacken'd, Man's Forgiveness give and take ! "

In the second edition three new stanzas were prefixed to the two above quoted :—

> " What ! out of senseless Nothing to provoke
>   A conscious Something to resent the yoke
>   Of unpermitted Pleasure, under pain
>   Of Everlasting Penalties, if broke !

> What ! from his helpless Creature be repaid
>   Pure Gold for what he lent us dross-allay'd—,
>   Sue for a Debt we never did contract
>   And cannot answer—oh the sorry trade !

> Nay, but, for terror of his wrathful Face,
> I swear I will not call Injustice Grace ;
>   Not one Good Fellow of the Tavern but
> Would kick so poor a Coward from the place."

At the same time some alterations were made in the two stanzas of the first version; "Predestination" became "Predestin'd Evil."

The following line became :—

> "Enmesh, and then impute my fall to Sin."

In stanza lviii., 'who with Eden didst' became 'and ev'n with Paradise'; and the second couplet was altered, decidedly for the worse, to :—

> "For all the Sin the Face of wretched Man
> Is black with—Man's Forgiveness give, and take !"

But in the third edition the original form of the couplet was replaced and retained. At the same time the quatrain, "Nay, but, for terror, etc.," was eliminated by a very true instinct. The image of the Coward being kicked from the tavern is altogether below the dignity of the vein.

It seems that the startling line—

> "And ev'n with Paradise devise the Snake"—

is based again upon an apologue of Attar's, and does not occur in Omar.

Professor Cowell says that the majestic line—

> "Man's Forgiveness give, *and take*"—

is a simple misapprehension, arising from the fact that FitzGerald thought a contrast was intended in the original line—

> "Thou who *grantest* repentance and *acceptest* excuses"—

which was not really intended by the writer. "I wrote to him about it when I was in Calcutta," he added, "but he never cared to alter it." But it is even more probable that FitzGerald had in his mind a quatrain which he translates in an unpublished letter, "O God, forgive when I repent, and I will forgive when Thou repentest."

Perhaps the finest of all the transformations in the poem is to be found in the two stanzas which sum up the stern and dark philosophy that man is the measure of all things :—

> " I sent my soul through the Invisible,
>   Some letter of that After-life to spell :
>   And by-and-by my soul returned to me,
>   And answered, ' I myself am Heav'n and Hell :
>
> Heav'n but the Vision of fulfill'd Desire,
> And Hell the shadow from a Soul on fire,
>   Cast on the Darkness into which Ourselves,
> So late emerged from, shall so soon expire.' "

" Already," says Omar, " on the day of Creation, beyond the heavens, my soul

> " Searched for the Tablet and Pen,[1] for heaven and hell ;
>   At last the Teacher said to me with His enlightened judgment,
> Tablet and Pen, and heaven and hell, are within thyself.
>
> The heavenly vault is a girdle (cast) from my weary body.
> Jihun (Oxus) is a watercourse worn by my filtered tears,
> Hell is a spark from my useless worries,
> Paradise is a moment of time when I am tranquil." [2]

And perhaps the line of Attar, " Heaven and hell are reflections, the one of Thy goodness and the other of Thy wrath," lends a sidelight to the stanza.

What is notable in FitzGerald's version is that he has caught the central thought, and both simplified and amplified it. He has discarded several beautiful

---

[1] "Tablet and Pen" are the Divine decrees of fate.

[2] Translated by Mr. E. Heron-Allen.

Oriental touches, such as that in the first stanza of Omar, that the quest has been from all time; and in the second, that even the rivers of earth take their part in the sad fellowship. But here in FitzGerald the vesture of the soul is torn aside, and the spirit, at once timorous and indomitable, is revealed in its utter nakedness; and the terrifying thought added that, so far as knowledge can go, the very perception of the deepest things of the world can only be the unconfirmed inference of the single soul.

The story of the publication and reception of the book are too curious to be omitted. FitzGerald sent the manuscript to *Fraser's Magazine* in 1858. Almost exactly a year later, in 1859, as the poem did not appear, he demanded its return, and published it in a small quarto in a brown wrapper, the price five shillings. Two hundred and fifty copies were printed. He sent a few to his friends, and the rest he gave to Quaritch. The history of their "discovery" is as follows.

Mr. Swinburne says :—

"Two friends of Rossetti's—Mr. Whitley Stokes and Mr. Ormsby—told him (he told me) of this wonderful little pamphlet for sale on a stall in St. Martin's Lane, to which Mr. Quaritch, finding that the British public unanimously declined to give a shilling for it, had relegated it to be disposed of for a penny. Having read it, Rossetti and I invested upwards of sixpence apiece—or possibly threepence —I would not wish to exaggerate our extravagance—in copies at that not exorbitant price. Next day we thought we might get some more for presents among our friends, but the man at the stall asked twopence ! Rossetti expostulated with him in terms of such humorously indignant remonstrance as none but he could ever have commanded. We took a few, and left him. In a week or two, if I am not much mistaken, the remaining copies were sold at a guinea ; I have since—as I dare say you have—seen copies offered for still more absurd prices. I kept my pennyworth (the tidiest copy of the lot), and have it still."

FitzGerald's own account of the motives which induced him to publish the book is as follows. He wrote to Cowell :—

"I sent you poor old *Omar*, who has *his* kind of Consolation for all these Things. I doubt you will regret you ever introduced him to me. And yet you would have me print the original, with many worse things than I have translated. The Bird Epic might be finished at once : but *cui bono* ? No one cares for such things ; and there are doubtless so many better things to care about. I hardly know why I print any of these things, which nobody buys ; and I·scarce now see the few I give them to. But when one has done one's best, and is sure that that best is better than so many will take pains to do, though far from the best that *might be done*, one likes to make an end of the matter by Print. I suppose very few People have ever taken such Pains in Translation as I have ; though certainly not to be literal. But at all Cost, a Thing must *live* : with a transfusion of one's own worse Life if one can't retain the Original's better. Better a live Sparrow than a stuffed Eagle. I shall be very well pleased to see the new MS. of *Omar*. I shall *one day* (if I live) print the *Birds*, and a strange experiment on old Calderon's two great Plays ; and then shut up Shop in the Poetic Line."

Again, almost at the end of his life, he wrote a long letter on the whole subject, which is interesting :—

"In Omar's case it was different : he sang, in an acceptable way it seems, of what all men feel in their hearts, but had not had exprest in verse before : Jámí tells of what everybody knows, under cover of a not very skilful Allegory. I have undoubtedly improved the whole by boiling it down to about a Quarter of its original size ; and there are many pretty things in it, though the blank Verse is too Miltonic for Oriental style.

"All this considered, why did I ever meddle with it? Why, it was the first Persian Poem I read, with my friend Edward Cowell, near on forty years ago; and I was so well pleased with it then (and now think it almost the best of the Persian Poems I have read or heard about) that I published my Version of it in 1856 (I think) with Parker of the Strand. When Parker disappeared, my unsold Copies, many more than of the sold, were returned to me, some of which, if not all, I gave to little Quaritch, who, I believe, trumpeted them off to some little profit; and I thought no more of them.

"But some six or seven years ago that Sheikh of mine, Edward Cowell, who liked the Version better than any one else, wished it to be reprinted. So I took it in hand, boiled it down to three-fourths of what it originally was, and (as you see) clapped it on the back of Omar, where I still believed it would hang somewhat of a dead weight; but that was Quaritch's look-out, not mine. I have never heard of any notice taken of it, but just now from you; and I believe that, say what you would, people would rather have the old Sinner alone. Therefore it is that I write all this to you. I doubt not that any of your Editors would accept an Article from you on the Subject, but I believe also they would much prefer one on many another Subject; and so, probably, with the Public whom you write for.

"Thus *liberavi animam meam* for your behoof, as I am rightly bound to do in return for your Goodwill to me."

In a rather more humorous vein, he had written twenty years before to W. H. Thompson :—

"As to my own Peccadilloes in Verse, which never pretend to be original, this is the story of Rubáiyát. I had translated them partly for Cowell; young Parker asked me some years ago for something for *Fraser*, and I gave him the less wicked of these to use as he chose. He kept them for two years without using; and as I saw he didn't want them, I printed some copies with Quaritch; and keeping some for myself, gave him the rest. Cowell, to whom I sent a copy, was naturally alarmed at it, he being a very religious Man:

nor have I given any other Copy but to George Borrow . . .
and to old Donne. . . ."

The fame of the book was at first secret, and con-
fined συνετοῖσιν. Not until nine years had passed was
a second edition published. The first edition contained
only seventy-five quatrains, the second one hundred
and ten, the third and fourth, which were the only
later ones published in the author's lifetime, one hundred and one. Since then it has gone through many
editions both in England and America. It is one of
the rare cases of a work of supreme merit escaping
notice at first; but a proof of its originality is the fact
that the metre appears to be consecrated by right to
FitzGerald : it is like the *In Memoriam* stanza ; it seems
impossible to use either of these metres without appearing to imitate the original ; it would seem as if the
metre could only be used in a particular way, and with
a particular style. Yet the *Omar* has been extensively
imitated.

> " All can raise the flower now,
>   For all have got the seed."

What FitzGerald saw in Omar was rather his difference from the other Oriental poets with whom he was
himself acquainted, than his likeness to them. While
most Eastern poetry tends to lose itself in vague imagery, more or less relevant to the matter in hand,
Omar, he thought, had a certain concentration of
thought, a definite conception which he endeavoured to
indicate. On this point FitzGerald wrote to Cowell :—

"I shall look directly for the passages in Omar and Hafiz
which you refer to, and clear up, though I scarce ever see the
Persian Character now. I suppose you would think it a dangerous thing to edit Omar ; else, who so proper? Nay, are
you not the only Man to do it? And he certainly is worth
good re-editing. I thought him from the first the most

remarkable of the Persian Poets ; and you keep finding out in him Evidences of logical Fancy which I had not dreamed of. I dare say these logical Riddles are not his best ; but they are yet evidences of a Strength of mind which our Persian Friends rarely exhibit, I think. I always said about Cowley, Donne, etc., whom Johnson calls the metaphysical Poets, that their very Quibbles of Fancy showed a power of Logic which could follow Fancy through such remote Analogies. This is the case with Calderon's Conceits also. I doubt I have given but a very one-sided version of Omar ; but what I do only comes up as a Bubble to the Surface, and breaks ; whereas you, with exact Scholarship, might make a lasting impression of such an Author."

Much has been written about the symbolism of Omar. Literary persons, more careful than himself of the old poet's delicacy, have tried to prove that the imagery of the poem, like that of the Song of Solomon, is of a spiritual and symbolic character. In one sense, indeed, all art has a symbolical side; a poem and a picture are nothing if they are not typical, if they are not, so to speak, a blank cheque upon the emotions, which those that come after may fill up according to their desires and their emotional capacity. But just as the VENI SPONSA DE LIBANO, VENI, CORO-NABERIS, though mystically applied by the high-minded to the invitation of Christ to his Church, was based upon a far more passionate, if less exalted dream ; so it is impossible to believe that when Omar wrote of the joys of the cup and the scented tresses of the cypress-slender minister of wine, he was speaking in allegories of remote visions and spiritual ecstasies. Perhaps he did not write his momentary experiences, perhaps his dreams were emotionally recollected, looking back in his wistful age upon "youth and strength and this delightful world." But there is no doubt that Omar must have drunk his fill of bodily delights ; he speaks of these things in no veiled allegories, but even, in stanzas which FitzGerald shunned, in terms of unmistakable grossness. No one could have written as Omar who had not felt the flush of the juice of the vine stir and excite the languid thought, as the returning tide sets afloat the fringes of the seaweed. No one could have written as Omar did of love who had not thrilled spell-bound at the sight of some beloved face touching into life those hungering, incommunicable dreams. The master had suffered himself, though he pursued his lonely way past those sweet visions, out from the garden with its rose-twined shelters and bubbling fountains into the sand-ridged desert that lies in its hot desolation all about the sheltered pleasaunce. Like the author of Ecclesiastes, who had seen "the emptiness and horror of the dark" that lay so close to the door of joy, Omar was full of desolation at the bitter mystery. But unlike the author of Ecclesiastes, unlike the Stoic and the Christian moralist, he had not the heart to preach detachment. He could not adopt the view that because these delights are transitory, therefore they must be resolutely avoided. Rather he clung to them, in the spirit of the later poet :—

> "But oh, the very reason why
> I clasp them, is *because* they die."

That these things should be so sweet and yet so brief was to Omar, as to FitzGerald, the heart of the mystery ; not a thought to be banished or to be replaced by some far-off hope, but a thought to be dealt with, to be wreathed with flowers, and to be made musical, if that might be.

"Did I not once," wrote the author of the above pathetic lines, as he sat beside a summer sea, breaking in a golden-sanded bay, "did I not once—surely I did

—enjoy like a lover the first sight of a sunny bay? and now I cannot think of it without heartache." And again, after "a day of sad and kindly partings," he wrote, "What a world it is for sorrow. And how dull it would be if there were no sorrow." That is the mood of Omar, and that, chastened and refined by a sweeter and more generous nature, is the mood of FitzGerald.

Cowell, writing of Omar in the *Calcutta Review,* said :—

"His tetrastichs are filled with bitter satires of the sensuality and hypocrisy of the pretenders to sanctity, but he did not stop there. He could see with a clear eye the evil and folly of the charlatans and empirics ; but he was blind when he turned from these, to deny the existence of the soul's disease, or, at any rate, of the possibility of a cure. Here, like Lucretius, he cut himself loose from facts ; and in both alike we trace the unsatisfied instincts,—the dim conviction that their wisdom is folly,—which reflect themselves in darker colours in the misanthropy and despair, which cloud their visions of life."

But FitzGerald felt that Cowell could not quite put himself in line with the thought of the poem :—

"You see all his beauty," he wrote, "but you don't feel *with* him in some respects as I do."

As to the *motif* of the poem, FitzGerald himself sums up in a sad and tender epigram, as far as so evasive a thing can be summarised, the underlying thought. In 1877, sending the book to his friend Laurence, he wrote: "I know you will thank me (for the book), and I think you will feel a sort of *triste Plaisir* in it, as others besides myself have felt. *It is a desperate sort of thing, unfortunately at the bottom of all thinking men's minds ; but made Music of.*"

To translate that exquisite sentence into more

scientific and harsher terminology, the poem is probably the most beautiful and stately presentation of Agnosticism ever made, with its resultant Epicureanism. Omar does not go to the wine-jar only that he may forget, but that he may also remember. He feeds on honey-dew and drinks the milk of paradise that he may banish for a little the terror of the unknown, the bewildered mystery of life, the pain, the shame, the fear, and the dark shadow that nearer or further lies across the road; thus much to forget; and then he is, perchance, enabled to remember the sweet days, the spring and the budding rose; to remember that though the beginning and the end are dark, yet that the God of Pain and Death is also the maker of the fair world, the gracious charm of voice and hand and eye, the woven tapestry of tree and meadow-grass, the sunset burning red behind the dark tree-trunks of the grove, the voice of music, the song of the bird, the whisper of leaves, the murmur of the hidden stream— of all the sights and sounds that fill the heart full and leave it yearning, unsatisfied with the pain that is itself a joy.

And, then, in such a mood the shadow of loss, the memory of sweet things that have an end, the sleep of death, tremble into music too; and are like the deep, slow pedal-notes above which the lighter descant wings its way, as a bird that flies dipping its feet in the slow-stirring wave.

All is vanity; that is the low cry of the tired heart when the buoyant strength of youth dies away, and when the brave shows of the glittering world, the harsh inspiriting music of affairs, the ambition to speak and strive, to sway hearts and minds or destinies, fade into the darkness of the end. Against the assaults of this nameless fear men hold out what shields they can ; the shield of honour, the shield of labour, and, best of all, the shield of faith. But there are some who have found no armour to help them, and who can but sink to the ground, covering their face beneath the open eye of heaven, and say with FitzGerald, "It is He that hath made us," resigning the mystery into the hands of the power that formed us and bade us be. For behind the loud and confident voice of work and politics and creeds there must still lurk the thought that whatever aims we propose to ourselves, though they be hallowed with centuries of endeavour and con- secration, we cannot know what awaits us or what we shall be. We strive to believe in Justice and Mercy, in love and purity ; and nature, which is still the work of God, gives us the lie a hundred times over ; till the shrinking soul asks itself, "Am I indeed trying to be better, purer, more just than the God who made me ? Am I thus forced to fall, to be a traitor to my secret desire for virtue, and then to be sternly punished for doing what I had not the strength to escape ?" Such thoughts may not be uplifting or inspiring, but they are there ; so that a man in this dark valley feels him- self to be, indeed, the sport of a vast power who holds out the cup of joy and dashes it from the lip, who makes alike the way of the saint and the sinner to be hard.

Perhaps the best medicine that can be given to a spirit thus brought face to face with the hardest and darkest truth is that he should fix his thought firmly on the grace and beauty so abundantly shed abroad in the world. Not thus, indeed, can the whole victory be won, the victory of the troubled spirit that can say, "Though He slay me, yet will I trust in Him" ; but the message of beauty may form as it were the first firm steps by which the soul can climb a little way

out of the abyss.   The peril is that the spirit may have
no strength to climb further, and may loiter with Omar
in the wilderness, greedy of transient delights, content
with the strip of herbage that fringes the desert,
putting off the pilgrimage.

It is not to be feared that this subtle murmuring
voice out of the East will win any notable influence in
the busy world of the West.   Yet it is strange how
we have transmuted that other mightier Eastern voice,
the message of the Gospel, to serve our own ideals and
to justify what it set out to condemn.

CHAPTER VI

OF the plays to the translation of which FitzGerald
devoted so much time and thought, there is much that
might be said. But the plain truth is, however melancholy a confession it is to make, that they are not
really worth a very critical examination. We need
not exactly regret the labour he spent upon them,
because it was through such exercises that FitzGerald
gained the command of stately diction that enabled
him to seize the one supreme chance that fell in his
way. But they are nothing more than good and
careful literary work; here and there rising, in certain
passages and single lines, into stateliness and beauty.
Any one who is interested in FitzGerald is glad to
have the opportunity of seeing how his mind worked;
but the plays have no permanent or intrinsic merit such
as belongs to the *Omar* and the Letters.

FitzGerald's theory of such versions as he made is
best given in his own words, in the Preface which he
prefixed to the *Agamemnon.*

"Thus," he writes, ". . . this grand play, which, to the
scholar and the poet, lives, breathes and moves in the dead
language, has hitherto seemed to me to drag and stifle under
conscientious translation into the living; that is to say, to
have lost that which I think the drama can least afford to lose
all the world over. And so it was that, hopeless of succeeding
where as good versifiers, and better scholars, seemed to me to
have failed, I came first to break the bounds of Greek

118

Tragedy ; then to swerve from the Master's footsteps ; and so, one licence drawing on another to make all of a piece, arrived at the present anomalous conclusion. If it has succeeded in shaping itself into a distinct, consistent and animated Whole, through which the reader can follow without halting, and not without accelerating interest from beginning to end, he will perhaps excuse my acknowledged transgressions, and will not disdain the Jade which has carried him so far so well till he finds himself mounted on a Thorough-bred whose thunder-clothed neck and long-resounding pace shall better keep up with the Original."

His general principle of translation was as follows :—

" Well, I have not turned over Johnson's Dictionary for the last month, having got hold of Æschylus. I think I want to turn his Trilogy into what shall be readable English Verse ; a thing I have always thought of, but was frightened at the Chorus. So I am now ; I can't think them so fine as People talk of : they are terribly maimed ; and all such Lyrics require a better Poet than I am to set forth in English. But the better Poets won't do it ; and I cannot find one readable translation. I shall (if I make one) make a very free one ; not for Scholars, but for those who are ignorant of Greek, and who (so far as I have seen) have never been induced to learn it by any Translations yet made of these Plays. I think I shall become a bore, of the Bowring order, by all this Translation : but it amuses me without any labour, and I really think I have the faculty of making some things readable which others have hitherto left unreadable."

But the result of this principle has been that Fitz-Gerald gives but little idea of the original. Half the charm, so to speak, of these ancient human documents is their authenticity. Not only the archaic form, the statuesque conventionality of the Greek stage, the traditions of a once-living art, are sacrificed ; but, what is more important still, the very spirit of Greek Tragedy, the unshrinking gaze into the darkest horrors of life, the dreadful insistence of Fate, forcing men to tread unwillingly in rough and stony paths—these are thrown aside. And thus the force, the grim tension, which are of the essence of Greek tragedy are replaced by a species of gentle dignity, which leaves the stiffness of movement without the compensating strength, and the austere frigidity without the antique spirit. A kind of flowing and even Shakespearian diction takes the place of the gorgeousness of the original, but without any of the modern flexibility of handling.

It seems that there are two possibilities open to the translator: the first, to make a literal and dignified version, which is probably better in prose, of the kind of which Sir Richard Jebb has produced masterly specimens. There indeed you are probably as near to the ancient Greek as without a knowledge of the language you can get. Or else, to produce a frankly modern play, just following the lines of the ancient drama, and endeavouring to represent movement and emotion rather than language. FitzGerald has fallen between these two possibilities. The plays are frigid but not archaic; timid where the ancient plays were bold; gentlemanly where the originals were noble. They are as like Greek plays as the Eglinton Tournament was like a mediæval Joust; a revival in which the spirit, the only thing which justified and enlivened the ancient sport, has somehow evaporated.

In the version of the *Œdipus*, FitzGerald allows himself great licence, but in the *Agamemnon* his method is still more luxuriant. For instance, when the Herald from the host describes the miseries of the life of the camp, he says:—

　　" Not the mere course and casualty of war,
　　Alarum, March, Battle, and such hard knocks

As foe with foe expects to givean d take;
But all the complement of miseries
That go to swell a long campaign's account,
Cramm'd close aboard the ships, hard bed, hard board :
Or worse perhaps while foraging ashore
In winter time ; when, if not from the walls,
Pelted from Heav'n by Day, to couch by Night
Between the falling dews and rising damps
That elf'd the locks, and set the body fast
With cramp and ague ; or, to mend the matter
Good mother Ida from her winter top
Flinging us down a coverlet of snow.
Or worst perhaps in Summer, toiling in
The bloody harvest-field of torrid sand,
When not an air stirr'd the fierce Asian noon
And even the sea sleep-sicken'd in his bed."

There is no doubt that this is a fine passage   But
what is the source of it ?—

"For if I were to tell of the toils and the hard quarters,
the narrow ill-strewn berths—nay, what day-long privation
too did we not have to bewail ? and then again on land—where
danger was ever at hand, for we couched close by the walls—
from heaven and earth alike the meadow dews down-drizzling
crept, the constant rotting of our raiment, breeding evil
vermin in our very hair ; and if one were to tell of the winter
that slew the birds themselves, the intolerable cold that the
snows of Ida brought, or the heat, when the unstirred ocean
fell and slept in his windless bed." [1]

Perhaps it is ill to quarrel with a method deliberately
adopted; but it will be seen that it ends in a mere
wrapping up of the ancient simplicities in an em-
broidered modern robe ; one who studies FitzGerald's
Agamemnon may do so for its own sake, but he must
not think that he is getting near either to the spirit or
the form of the original. It is idle to speculate to
what extent FitzGerald himself understood the Greek.

[1] *Ag.*, 560-571.

Even in the passage above quoted there are clear indications that he did not even penetrate the actual meaning; but on his principle, he might defend himself on the ground that he conceived the harshness of the images to be unsuited for modern taste.

This is still more noticeable in the lyrical translations of the choruses of the *Agamemnon*, in which FitzGerald seems to be hobbling in fetters, dealing with ideas and words that have no native existence in our own language except as pedantic attempts to represent in an English form thoughts which have no real counterpart in English thought. This terrible jargon, well-known to schoolmasters, this attempt to transvocalise, so to speak, Greek expressions, and to squeeze the juice out of the ancient language, strikes dreariness into the mind. Such a passage as the following from one of the grandest choruses will suffice to illustrate my meaning :—

> " But now to be resolved, whether indeed
>   Those fires of Night spoke truly, or mistold
>   To cheat a doating woman ; for behold
>   Advancing from the shore with solemn speed,
>   A Herald from the Fleet, his footsteps roll'd
>   In dust, Haste's thirsty consort, but his brow
>   Check-shadow'd with the nodding Olive-bough ;
>   Who shall interpret us the speechless sign
>   Of the fork'd tongue that preys upon the pine ? "

Who indeed? This passage is like a turbid stream in flood. It is muddy with Greek, it bears Greek particles, like river-wrack, floating on its surface. But it is neither Greek nor English. It can give no sense of pleasure to an English reader ; and to any one who can appreciate the original, it only brings a dim sense of pain.

The two versions of the *Œdipus* are even less satisfactory than the *Agamemnon* ; for there the serene and even flow of Sophocles' diction is converted into what it is difficult to distinguish from dulness. And here indeed FitzGerald has taken a licence which it is hard to condone; for he has transplanted entire into his pages the translation of the choruses by Robert Potter (1721-1804), in a mellifluous classical verse, of the school of Gray. "As I thought," he writes, "I should do no better with the Choruses than old Potter, I have left them, as you see, in his hands, though worthy of a better interpreter than either of us." And he has gone further still by practically omitting two of the principal characters in the two plays, Creon almost entirely in the first and Ismene entirely in the second, for no better reason than that the intrusion of characters whom he has the misfortune to dislike had appeared to him to be inartistic. And this is, I think, a really serious blot; because it is the very dissimilarity of the Greek point of view to our own, the different artistic standard, that contribute to give these plays their bewildering value. The whole essence of the culture which depends upon familiarising oneself with the best products of the human spirit, is that one should try to put oneself in line with the old. To admire a Greek play for the modernity which may be found in it, is, I believe, to misapprehend the situation altogether.

With regard to the omission of the character of Creon in two of the three scenes where he appears in the *Œdipus in Thebes* (*Tyrannus*), it may stand as a crucial instance of FitzGerald's methods. In the second scene Œdipus overwhelms Creon in a groundless charge of treason; but in spite of this Creon appears, in the third scene, in a mood of grave pity and magnanimous forbearance. He expresses a deep and sincere sympathy for the unhappy king; he receives

in a spirit of kindly benevolence the pathetic charge of
Œdipus that his unhappy daughters may be cared for.
He will not even bring himself to acquiesce in the
miserable man's entreaties that he may be banished
from the land, but says gravely that the oracle must
decide. Thus he plays a vital and integral part in the
play, and the contrast of his calm yet sorrowing dignity
with the terrible self-accusation of the ill-fated Œdipus
is not only intentional, but a lofty piece of art.

FitzGerald in the prefatory letter to the *Œdipus*
excuses himself airily for his omission, by saying that
from all this "little results except to show that the
Creon of this Play (the *Tyrannus*) proves himself by
his temperate self-defence, and subsequent forbearance
toward his accuser, very unlike the Creon of the two
after Tragedies" (the *Antigone* and the *Œdipus Coloneus*).
But the defence would only be valid if FitzGerald had
thrown the plot of the *Œdipus* overboard, and con-
structed a play of his own on the same plot. The
play in FitzGerald's hands simply ceases to represent
the original.

With regard to the Calderon plays we are on very
much the same ground. Calderon was essentially a
lyrical poet, and without being ungenerous to his art
it may be doubted whether, with all his mastery of
ingenious stage-craft, he was really altogether at home
in dramatic form.

However indulgently one may try to judge Fitz-
Gerald's versions of Calderon, they cannot be reckoned
among his literary successes. It is probable that
FitzGerald did not really understand Calderon, and
it is not unfair to say that we have here a marked
instance of FitzGerald's friendships biassing his studies.
It was no doubt the influence of Cowell that turned
his mind definitely to Calderon. It is probable that

Cowell did not introduce FitzGerald to Calderon, though he undoubtedly blew the smouldering ashes to a flame. England was full of Spanish liberals from 1823 to 1833. Archbishop Trench was a translator of Calderon, and Tennyson mentions Calderon in a suppressed stanza of *The Palace of Art*; so that it is probable that Calderon was not unknown in FitzGerald's Cambridge circle.

FitzGerald can hardly have cared instinctively for the Spanish dramatist, for it is impossible to conceive two temperaments that were more radically unlike. Calderon was a man of exemplary virtue; but he was a courtier to the fingers' ends. He enjoyed the splendid pageants, the gracious shows of life, and was a master of the arts of courtly living. What may be called his "profane" plays were chiefly written to please Philip IV., and to be acted at court performances. The plays—*autos*, as they are called—with a religious or "sacramental" motive [1] belong to a much higher order of genius. All this was entirely antipathetic to FitzGerald. Calderon was conventional, magnificent, worldly-minded, with a background of mysticism. FitzGerald hated conventionality in every form, clung to the simple and retired life, feared and hated the din of the great glittering world. Again, where Calderon was mystical, FitzGerald was agnostic. It is surely significant that in the 1853 volume, containing versions of six of Calderon's plays, FitzGerald admits that, with the exception of *The Mayor of Zalamea* (which is in reality a play of Lope's recast), none of Calderon's masterpieces are attempted. A man who could begin with the inferior works of the author he

---

[1] The *auto* is a species of mystical or allegorical play, based on the mediæval Mystery plays, and with the Eucharist for *motif*.

was translating could not have been greatly in earnest about his task. He did afterwards attempt two of the undoubted masterpieces, *The Mighty Magician* and *Beware of Smooth Water*; but these were an afterthought.

Again, it must be borne in mind that Calderon was a very artificial writer, and belonged to an extremely definite school. He abounds in preciosities and what may be called affectations both of manner and of thought. In the first place he is what would be called in English "Euphuistic"; his style is full of audacities and conceits, and of subtle refinements of thought. These are far from being the best part of Calderon; but the texture of his writings is so impregnated by them that they may be held to be absolutely essential to his style. FitzGerald omits and compresses, with the result that the airy grace and the fine elegance disappear; some of the poetry remains, but it is transposed into a different key; it is as when a bass sings a rearranged air intended for a tenor; it is quiet and homely instead of lustrous and brilliant. The result is that no one could really gain any idea of the characteristic manner of Calderon from Fitz-Gerald's version.

FitzGerald thus makes no pretence about the matter; he says frankly that he omitted these things because he did not care for them. But when we remember that Calderon cared for them, and that the whole Spanish nation cared for them, and that they represent an unbroken literary tradition of two centuries and a half, the confession is tantamount to saying that FitzGerald did not really care for Calderon. It remains then that by getting rid of what he called bombast, and recklessly throwing overboard unfamiliar idioms, FitzGerald is really shirking his most formidable difficulties.

As a rule he does not actually interpolate much, but rather touches up the lines by adding epithets and adverbs, doing what Gray called "sticking a flower in the buttonhole."

It is strange that FitzGerald was able to do the very thing for Omar that he could not do for Calderon : to seize and represent and even add intensity to the very essence of the writer.   But though Calderon has been called by so fine a critic as Lowell an Arab soul in Spanish feathers, it is a misapprehension.   There is nothing Oriental about Calderon.   He is a European, a modern, one of ourselves ; and it was precisely with the modern spirit that FitzGerald was not in sympathy, whereas he was to a considerable extent in sympathy with the Oriental spirit.   Again, the variety of metrical forms used in the Spanish drama is remarkable.   Calderon varies his measures with great skill and frequency, never sinking to prose ; and thus the effect of the blank verse with occasional rhyme endings, interspersed with a few lyrical passages and even many passages of plain prose, employed by Fitz-Gerald is misleading and monotonous.   Shelley's version of the *Magico Prodigioso* is far more Calderonian than anything in FitzGerald, and proves that to represent Calderon in English was not an altogether impossible task.

It may be noted that FitzGerald's knowledge of Spanish was very limited.   And again, it is clear that FitzGerald is very unsure about quantities, and that the accent shifts, in the proper names he uses, from syllable to syllable in a perplexing way.   This shows that he was not really very familiar with the language ; and lastly, it appears that he had frequent recourse to his dictionary even when reading Cervantes.   If this was so with Cervantes, it must

have been far more the case with Calderon, whose
vocabulary is much richer and more complex.   But
the conclusion that is forced upon us is that Fitz-
Gerald's equipment in Spanish was such as to make
it impossible for him to be an adequate interpreter
of a writer both intricate and difficult in a language
in which he was never really more than an enthusiastic learner.   These liberties and licences no doubt
account for the very unfavourable review which appeared in the *Athenæum*[1] of FitzGerald's translation.
The reviewer was John Rutter Chorley, one of the
best Spanish scholars that England has ever produced.
This review disconcerted FitzGerald extremely; but
Chorley was not quite just to his victim.   Indeed,
in an extract professedly quoted from FitzGerald,
Chorley, besides making two misquotations, actually
puts " ZALAMCA (*sic*)," thereby giving the impression
of the grossest carelessness on FitzGerald's part.
The original, it is true, is clumsily printed, so
that the letter *c* often resembles the letter *e*; yet
in this case FitzGerald gave the word correctly,
ZALAMEA.

The language employed by FitzGerald in the translation is a stately and flowing modern blank verse.
There is no sign that he aimed at imitating any
special English writer.   There is an occasional tendency to the use of rather recondite words and com-
binations such as " thrasonical," " mis-arrogates," but
as a rule he evidently tries to avoid anything that is
unusual or bizarre.   It is difficult, with the space at
my command, to give any idea of the style employed,
but I will quote one passage, where it is obvious that
great pains have been taken with the version, from
Such Stuff as Dreams are made of.   Segismund, the

[1] September 10, 1853, p. 1063, No. 1350, wrongly indexed.

King of Poland's son, has drunk the potion, and, still
fevered by the draught, soliloquises :—

> " SEGISMUND (*within*). . . . Forbear !   I stifle with your
>   perfume !   Cease
> Your crazy salutations !   Peace, I say—
> Begone, or let me go, ere I go mad
> With all this babble, mummery, and glare,
> For I am growing dangerous—Air ! room ! air !
>   (*He rushes in.   Music ceases.*)
> Oh, but to save this reeling brain from wreck
> With its bewildered senses !
>   (*He covers his eyes for a while.*)
>   What !   Ev'n now
> That Babel left behind me, but my eyes
> Pursued by the same glamour, that—unless
> Alike bewitch'd too—the confederate sense
> Vouches for palpable : bright-shining floors
> That ring hard answer back to the stamp'd heel,
> And shoot up airy columns marble-cold,
> That, as they climb, break into golden leaf
> And capital, till they embrace aloft
> In clustering flower and fruitage over walls
> Hung with such purple curtain as the West
> Fringes with such a gold ; or over-laid
> With sanguine-glowing semblances of men,
> Each in his all but living action busied,
> Or from the wall they look from, with fix'd eyes
> Pursuing me ; and one most strange of all
> That, as I pass'd the crystal on the wall,
> Look'd from it—left it—and as I return,
> Returns, and looks me face to face again—
> Unless some false reflection of my brain,
> The outward semblance of myself.—Myself ?
> How know that tawdry shadow for myself,
> But that it moves as I move ; lifts his hand
> With mine ; each motion echoing so close
> The immediate suggestion of the will
> In which myself I recognise—Myself !—
> What, this fantastic Segismund the same

I

Who last night, as for all his nights before,
Lay down to sleep in wolf-skin on the ground
In a black turret which the wolf howl'd round,
And woke again upon a golden bed,
Round which as clouds about a rising sun,
In scarce less glittering caparison,
Gather'd gay shapes that, underneath a breeze
Of music, handed him upon their knees
The wine of heaven in a cup of gold,
And still in soft melodious under-song
Hailing me Prince of Poland !—' Segismund,'
They said, ' Our Prince !   The Prince of Poland !' and
Again, ' Oh, welcome, welcome to his own,
Our own Prince Segismund.'"

Though it is plain that much literary skill has been
lavished on such lines as these, it must be confessed,
when all is said and done, that the plays cannot take high
rank as art.   We feel that it is neither FitzGerald nor
Calderon.   It is accomplished and stately, but there is
a want of dramatic sympathy, a want of fire and glow
for which no execution, however careful, can atone.

We must now turn to the only deliberately planned
and elaborately executed piece of prose which Fitz-
Gerald carried out.

The *Euphranor* is a pretty piece of delicate writing
cast in the mould of a dialogue of Plato.   The *dramatis
personæ* are four undergraduates, Euphranor, Lexilogus,
Lycion, and Phidippus, and the narrator, who is a
physician supposed to be practising at Cambridge,
nearly twice the age of his companions.   He is reading
a medical treatise in his room at Cambridge, when
Euphranor, a somewhat shadowy enthusiast, bursts in
upon him and insists upon his going by boat with him
to Chesterton.   They take with them Lexilogus, a
reclusive scholar, and the talk falls upon Chivalry, the

subject being suggested by Kenelm Digby's *Godefridus*,[1] a copy of which Euphranor carries with him. They reach Chesterton. Lexilogus goes off to call upon an elderly relative who lives there. The Protagonist and Euphranor go to the Three Tuns Inn, where they fall in with Lycion, a young man of fashion, who is something of a fop. They talk discursively, till Lycion goes away to play billiards. The others go for a walk, and fall in with Phidippus, who is riding, a cheerful, wholesome-minded, brisk young sportsman. They dine together, play bowls, and walk home in the cool of the evening. The sentiment that binds together the somewhat incongruous companions is that all the party, except Lycion, are Yorkshiremen.

The talk itself ranges discursively from chivalry to education, corporal punishment, and on to literature; the exact *motif* is somewhat difficult to disentangle. It reminds one of the criticism recorded to have been made by Jowett on the essay read to him by an enthusiastic undergraduate. Jowett heard it in silence; the subject, it must be said, was some precise one, such as the Eleatic School of Philosophy; but the writer had made the mistake of imagining that anything which came into his mind was relevant to the question under discussion. When the shrill tide of uninterrupted eloquence died away, Jowett said drily, "I do not observe that you have been following any particular line of thought."

The same impression prevails at the conclusion of the *Euphranor*; but it may be said generally that an attempt is made to arrive at a definition of the well-balanced and well-proportioned man, and of the value of physical strength and athletics in counterbalancing an undue amount of sensibility and imaginativeness.

[1] The first part of *The Broad Stone of Honour*.

Lycion and Phidippus seem to be introduced as types.
Lycion is intended, I believe, to be a figure resembling
Alcibiades, where the generous and natural impulses
of youth are vitiated by indolence and foppishness.
Phidippus, who is meant to be the most admirable
character in the dialogue, is the simple-hearted and
honest type of country gentleman, in whom the
physical side overbalances the intellectual. He was
confessedly drawn from FitzGerald's friend, W. K.
Browne. Lexilogus is no doubt a type of a nature
where there is an over-preponderance of the intellectual
element; but he is represented as a humble-minded and
ingenuous person. Euphranor is, of course, the hero,
impulsive, ardent, and impatient; while the Doctor acts
as a kind of genial and elderly moderator.

But the characters do not sufficiently reveal themselves in their talk, and the dramatic interest is small.
The conversation is a little heavy, somewhat man-
nerised, and neither quite idealistic or realistic enough.
One feels that the impatience of Lycion, who with-
draws from the talk in favour of a game of billiards, is
justified. "If I can't help being," he says with Platonic
petulance, "the very fine Fellow whom I think you were
reading about, I want to know what is the use of writing books about it for my edification."   The whole
tone is academical and frigid, and even the pleasantries,
which are carefully interspersed, are somewhat in the
style of Mr. Barlow.   "It is not easy," FitzGerald
wrote to Cowell when he was at work on the *Euphranor*,
"to keep to good dialectic, and yet keep up the dis-
jected sway of natural conversation. . . . Any such
trials of one's own show one the art of such dialogues
as Plato's, where the process is so logical and conversational at once. . . . They remain the miracles of that
Art to this day."

His own feeling about the book is well recorded in
another letter to Cowell:—

"Not but I think the Truth is told: only, a Truth every
one knows! And told in a shape of Dialogue really something
Platonic: but I doubt rather affectedly too. However, such
as it is, I send it you. I remember being anxious about it
twenty years ago, because I thought it was the Truth (as if my
telling it could mend the matter!); and I cannot but think
that the Generation that has grown up in these twenty years
has not profited by the Fifty Thousand Copies of this great
work!"

At the same time there are pleasant touches of
natural description throughout, such as "the new-
shaven expanse of grass," when they embark in the
Backs, "the Chestnut . . . in full fan, and leaning
down his white cones over the sluggish current, which
seems fitter for the slow merchandise of coal, than to
wash the walls and flow through the groves of Aca-
deme." And, again, there is the concluding passage
of the dialogue, so often quoted by those who praise
the little book that one is disposed to wonder whether
the reputation for beautiful style which it enjoys is
not mainly based upon the sentence. They walk
home "across the meadow leading to the town, whither
the dusky troops of Gownsmen with all their confused
voices seem'd as it were evaporating in the twilight,
while a Nightingale began to be heard among the
flowering Chestnuts of Jesus."

There are, too, charming passages about the poets
that come under discussion. The Canterbury Pilgrims
are described, "and one among them taking note of
all, in Verse still fresh as the air of those Kentish
hills they travelled over on that April morning four
hundred years ago."

Again, he writes of Wordsworth, that the strength

he had won by active exercise was so great "that he
may still be seen, I am told, at near upon Eighty,
travelling with the shadow of the cloud up Helvellyn."

Perhaps the most interesting passages are those that
refer to Tennyson, embodying anecdotes and *dicta*
which have since become familiar in biographies. Here
is a fine passage depicting Tennyson as he appeared in
the eye of his contemporaries. Euphranor is speaking
of the melancholy of Burns's "Ye Banks and Braes."

"Are you not forgetting," said I, "that Burns was not then
singing of himself, but of some forsaken damsel, as appears by
the second stanza? which few, by the way, care to remember.
As unremember'd it may have been," I continued after a pause,
"by the only living—and like to live—Poet I had known,
when, so many years after, he found himself beside that
'bonny Doon,' and—whether it were from recollection of poor
Burns, or of 'the days that are no more,' which haunt us all,
I know not—I think he did not know—but he somehow
'broke' as he told me, 'broke into a passion of tears.'—Of
tears which, during a pretty long and intimate intercourse, I
had never seen glisten in his eye but once, when reading
Virgil—'dear old Virgil,' as he call'd him—together; and
then of the burning of Troy in the second *Æneid*—whether
moved by the catastrophe's self, or the majesty of the Verse
it is told in—or, as before, scarce knowing why. For, as
King Arthur shall bear witness, no young Edwin he, though,
as a great Poet, comprehending all the softer stops of human
Emotion in that Register where the Intellectual, no less than
what is called the Poetical, faculty predominated. As all who
knew him know, a Man at all points, Euphranor, like your
Digby, of grand proportion and feature, significant of that
inward Chivalry, becoming his ancient and honourable race:
when himself a 'Yongé Squire,' like him in Chaucer 'of grete
strength,' that could hurl the crowbar further than any of the
neighbouring clowns, whose humours, as well as of their
betters—Knight, Squire, Landlord, and Land-tenant—he took
quiet note of, like Chaucer himself. Like your Wordsworth

on the Mountain, he too, when a Lad, abroad on the Wold;
sometimes of a night with the Shepherd; watching not only
the Flock on the greensward, but also

> " ' The fleecy Star that bears
> Andromeda far off Atlantic seas,'

along with those other Zodiacal constellations which Aries, I
think, leads over the field of Heaven. He then observed also
some of those uncertain phenomena of Night: unsurmised
apparitions of the Northern Aurora, by some shy glimpses
of which no winter—no, nor even summer—night, he said,
was utterly unvisited; and those strange voices, whether of
creeping brook, or copses muttering to themselves far off—
perhaps the yet more impossible Sea—together with 'other
sounds we know not whence they come,' says Crabbe, but all
inaudible to the ear of Day. He was not then, I suppose,
unless the Word spontaneously came upon him, thinking how
to turn what he saw and heard into Verse; a premeditation
that is very likely to defeat itself, previously breathing, as it
were, upon the mirror which is to receive the Image that most
assuredly flashes Reality into words."

Euphranor was published in 1851. FitzGerald was
not particularly proud of it, calling it "a pretty
specimen of a chiselled cherry-stone." He altered it a
good deal at a later date.

He seems at all events to have been thoroughly
in earnest when he wrote the dialogue; and it is
curious to consider how entirely the state of things that
it reflects has disappeared. It seems almost incredible
that fifty years ago it should have been necessary to
put in a plea for physical exercise at School and
College; that it should be necessary to plead that
Burns's poetry was no worse because he had followed
the plough, or that Gibbon's History was not vitiated
by his having been an officer in the Hampshire
Militia. If FitzGerald could now write a dialogue on
the subject of athletics, it is probable that he would

have delicately chastised the undue importance attached
to them.

Yet the little book remains, penetrated with the
delicate fragrance of a poetical spirit, with the strong
sense of beauty, and with the pathos of the brevity of
happiness, which was the dominant strain in Fitz-
Gerald's mind.

But it is not from the *Euphranor*, charming and
artistic as it is, that FitzGerald will win any perma-
nence of reputation.

Next to the *Omar Khayyám*, there is little doubt that
FitzGerald's best title to literary fame will be derived
from his letters.   The *Omar* forms, as it were, a
pedestal for his fame; without it FitzGerald's other
works would not have received, and, it may be frankly
said, would hardly have deserved attention.

But the statue, so to speak, which will stand upon
the pedestal, is the strange, remote, tender, wistful
personality which the letters reveal.   Indeed the
figure can hardly be said to stand; rather the easy,
unconsidered, natural pose recalls to the mind the *Sic
sedebat* of the statue of Bacon at Trinity College,
Cambridge.   There is no studied gesture, no draping
of honourable robes; but the man himself, with his
virtues and his faults, his strength and weakness,
beauty-loving, loyal, irresolute, and listless, is before
you as he lived.

The one condition that makes letters memorable is
that they should reveal personality.   But in England,
we are so enamoured of definite achievement that we
scarcely care to read the letters of any except those
who have won for themselves a fame in other regions.
It might be that one who desired to tread a new path of
literary renown could devote himself with a single eye
to letter-writing.   But there are several disadvantages

attending the practice. The first is that any renown
attainable is almost bound to be posthumous; and there
are few literary men who could so put away the desire
for contemporary fame as to pour their mind and
heart into the task. Then, again, the fame of a letter-
writer is at the mercy of accidents; his correspondents
may not preserve the documents. It is possible to
do as Pope and J. A. Symonds did, and preserve copies
of letters, even to annotate them for future publication.
But this is to make the business a pompous one, and to
wipe off the bloom which is half the delight of beautiful letters, the bloom of a careless naturalness.

FitzGerald's letters will please by a sort of confiding
and childlike wistfulness, which is never undignified,
combined with a delicate humour, a shrewd eye for
all that is characteristic, an admirable power of brief
and picturesque description, and by a style which is at
once familiar and stately. The earlier letters have
more stateliness than the latter, and the only sign of
youth in them is a sort of deliberate quaintness and
even pomposity, which fell away from him in his later
years. His letters, like Charles Lamb's, are full of
echoes, echoes of books and voices and the sweet sounds
of nature. The letters are never dull; even the most
detailed and domestic have that evasive quality called
charm; and the style, though it is seldom elaborate,
always walks with a certain daintiness and precision.
There are many little mannerisms in the letters, which,
like all mannerisms, please if the personality pleases.
Such are FitzGerald's use of initial capitals to indicate
emphatic substantives—"I like plenty of Capitals," he
used to say—and his unique punctuation, which brings
the very gradations of voice and pauses of thought
before the reader. Both of these mannerisms were
taken, I believe, to a great extent from Crabbe.

FitzGerald's management of paragraphs is another
salient characteristic; and he has, moreover, a peculiar
delicacy in his use of paragraph endings, which close
the passage as it were with a certain snap, leaping
briskly from the page, instead of dying feebly away
into silence.

Again, FitzGerald's handling of anecdote is another
salient characteristic of his style.   Nowadays letter-
writers are, as a rule, far too much in a hurry to deal
in anecdotes.   But FitzGerald tells a story with
delighted zest, repeating it to different correspondents
frequently.   He had, too, a marvellous sense of pathos;
not the superficial pathos which depends upon accidents, but the pathos which has its root in the *lacrimæ
rerum.*

Being confidential by temperament, FitzGerald
needed some one to confess to, to gossip to, to be sad
or merry with, according to his mood.   He wrote
to Allen in 1832 :—

"I am of that superior race of men, that are quite content
to hear themselves talk, and read their own writing.   But, in
seriousness, I have such love of you, and of myself, that once
every week, at least, I feel spurred on by a sort of gathering
up of feelings to vent myself in a letter upon you : but if
once I hear you say that it makes your conscience thus uneasy
till you answer, I shall give it up.   Upon my word, I tell you,
that I do not in the least require it.   You, who do not love
writing, cannot think that any one else does : but I am sorry
to say that I have a very young-lady-like partiality to writing
to those that I love. . . ."

But beside the humanity of the letters there is a
grateful sense of leisureliness about them.   These
letters are not written in the train, like the letters of
eminent Bishops, nor dashed off against time, as by
statesmen waiting to keep an appointment; they are

rather written gently and equably in the firelit room, with the curtains drawn, and the cat purring beside the hearth ; or in the pleasant summer, with the windows open, and the scent of roses in the air. They are not written with any motive, except to have a confidential talk with an absent friend ; and, what is one of the greatest charms of good letters, they are not written *to* a correspondent but *from* the writer. They are not replies ; but with a gentle egotism, they give picture after picture of the simple life FitzGerald was leading. They preserve the moment, the hour, the scene ; they indicate the thought just as it rose fresh in the author's mind. I imagine that FitzGerald had one special felicity in framing these letters ; he was not a conversationalist of a high order ; his reflective mind did not move briskly enough. But one cannot resist the feeling that his mind worked exactly as fast as he wrote ; the thought never outruns the expression : the expression never lags behind the thought.

Another great charm of the letters is their inimitable humour ; it is not wit in FitzGerald's case so much as a subtle, permeating medium which penetrates a whole passage and lends it a delicate aroma. It is difficult to give instances of a quality which, as it were, rather soaks a whole letter than gathers at salient points ; but I select a few short passages.

Thus, in one of his most delightful letters to Barton, he describes with humorous pomposity an invitation he had received to give a lecture :—

"If I do not see you before I go to London, I shall assuredly be down again by the latter part of February ; when toasted cheese and ale shall again unite our souls. You need not however expect that I can return to such familiar intercourse as once (in former days) passed between us. New honours in society have devolved upon me the

necessity of a more dignified deportment. A letter has been
sent from the Secretary of the Ipswich Mechanics' Institution
asking me to Lecture—any subject but Party Politics or
Controversial Divinity. On my politely declining, another,
a fuller, and a more pressing letter was sent urging me to
comply with their demand : I answered to the_same effect,
but with accelerated dignity. I am now awaiting the third
request in confidence : if you see no symptoms of its being
mooted, perhaps you will kindly propose it. I have prepared
an answer. Donne is mad with envy."

And when was ever so much colour and rhetoric ex-
pended on a question of poultry ?

"It occurs to me that, when I last saw you, you gave me
hopes of finding a *Chanticleer* to replace that aged fellow you
saw in my Domains. *He* came from Grundisburgh ; and
surely you spoke of some such Bird flourishing in Grundisburgh still. I will not hold out for the identical plumage—
worthy of an Archangel—I only stipulate for one of the sort :
such as are seen in old Story books ; and on Church-vanes ;
with a plume of Tail, a lofty Crest and Walk, and a shrill
trumpet-note of Challenge : and splendid colours ; black and
red ; black and Gold ; white, and red, and Gold ! Only so
as he be 'gay,' according to old Suffolk speech.

"Well, of course you won't trouble yourself about this :
only don't *forget* it, next time you ride through Grundisburgh. Or if, in the course of any Ride, you should see any
such Bird, catch him up at once upon your Saddle-bow, and
bring him to the distressed Widows on my Estate."

Or he could describe with humorous perception
the foibles even of those whom he devotedly loved.
He wrote to Mrs. Kemble :—

"I have been having Frederic Tennyson with me down
here. He has come to England (from Jersey where his home
now is) partly on Business, and partly to bring over a deaf
old Gentleman who has discovered the Original Mystery of
Freemasonry, by means of Spiritualism. The Freemasons
have for Ages been ignorant, it seems, of the very Secret

which all their Emblems and Signs refer to : and the question is, if they care enough for their own Mystery to buy it of this ancient Gentleman. If they do not, he will shame them by Publishing it to all the world. Frederic Tennyson, who has long been a Swedenborgian, a Spiritualist, and is now even himself a Medium, is quite grand and sincere in this as in all else : with the Faith of a Gigantic Child—pathetic and yet humorous to consider and consort with."

The following is not a criticism—only a Shake-spearian handling of gossip :—

"Have you heard that Arthur Malkin is to be married ? to a Miss Carr, with what Addison might call a pleasing fortune : or perhaps Nicholas Rowe. ' Sweet, pleasing friendship, etc. etc.' Mrs. Malkin is in high spirits about it, I hear : and I am very glad indeed. God send that you have not heard this before : for a man likes to be the first teller of a pretty piece of news."

One of the special powers which FitzGerald possessed as a letter-writer is his capacity to touch off a little vignette of a scene : these tiny pictures are like Bewick translated into prose, simple, homely, even fantastic, but always just suffused with a sentiment, a tender emotion. Such is the picture he draws of the old English Manor-house, holding up its *inquiring* chimneys and weathercocks, which could be espied by sailors out on the restless sea, or his cottage thatch perforated by lascivious sparrows, or the white clouds moving over the new-fledged tops of oak-trees.

Here is a little sketch of a windy night in the marshy flats of Woodbridge :—

"Three nights ago I looked out at about ten o'clock at night, before going to bed. It seemed perfectly still ; frosty, and the stars shining bright. I heard a continuous moaning sound, which I knew to be, not that of an infant exposed, or female ravished, but of the sea, more than ten miles off ! What little wind there was carried to us the murmurs of the

wave circulating round these coasts so far over a flat country.
But people here think that this sound so heard is not from the
waves that break, but a kind of prophetic voice from the body
of the sea itself announcing great gales. . . ."

Here is a tiny characterisation of the Oleander :—

" Don't you love the Oleander ?   So clean in its leaves and
stem, as so beautiful in its flower ; loving to stand in water,
which it drinks up so fast.   I rather worship mine."

Here he sits, in a dry month, old and blind, being
read to by a country boy, longing for rain :—

" Last night when Miss Tox was just coming, like a good
Soul, to ask about the ruined Dombey, we heard a Splash of
Rain, and I had the Book shut up, and sat listening to the
Shower by myself—till it blew over, I am sorry to say, and
no more of the sort all night.   But we are thankful for that
small mercy."

Again, another delight of these letters is the full-
furnished mind out of which they proceeded.   Fitz-
Gerald's brain was like the magic isle—

" Full of noises,
Sounds and sweet airs, that give delight and hurt not."

The old music of bygone singers, rich haunting
sentences of old leisurely authors, rang in his brain,
and came unbidden to his pen.

Then, too, there is a great plenty of the finest
critical appreciation throughout the letters.   His
friendship with Professor Norton, near the end of
his life, seems to have called this faculty out with
especial prodigality.   I suppose that with his old
and intimate friends FitzGerald thought that his
literary preferences and critical judgments might
have a certain air of familiarity.   But to this apprecia-
tive stranger from the new world he opened his mind,

and, like the wise householder, brought out of his treasure things new and old.

FitzGerald had, too, another characteristic which stood him in good stead; he was innately and by training a great gentleman; and thus he never complains. He admits his correspondent by swift and humorous touches into his troubles and little afflictions; but always with a kind of gentle contempt for his own weakness in being vexed by such slight annoyances. He was very fond of the story of the rich gentleman whom John Wesley visited, who, when the chimney smoked, cried out with Christian resignation, "These are some of the crosses, Mr. Wesley, that I have to bear." FitzGerald disliked obtruding his own afflictions. He felt them with an increasing impatience, but he never inflicts them upon his correspondent; he never airs a grievance.

Of his graver sorrows he hardly dares to speak. Again and again he closes the door upon grief with a kind of noble and Stoical resignation. Yet the result is that the reader of the letters feels that he is being confided in; he never loses the sense of *intimité*, while at the same time he is never bored by a want of perspective.

FitzGerald had, moreover, a very true and instinctive judgment of people. He had many weaknesses of his own, but he was acutely observant of the foibles of others. And he had, too, the spectatorial power of extracting a kind of critical pleasure out of salient indications of personality. And all this with a lightness of touch which never presses hard upon a delicate effect, never degenerates into tediousness or twaddle.

Of course the letters will not suit every one. Readers who are in search of definite facts and definite anecdotes, who prefer precise scandal about historical personages to subtle revelations of character and personality, may think there is much sauce and little meat. But FitzGerald's letters, though they contain interesting incidental reminiscences of distinguished persons, will be read more for the subtle aroma which pervades them than as solid contributions to the literary history of the time. He himself set no great value on his letters. "I don't think letter-writing men are much worth," he wrote to Lowell in 1878. Yet, if only FitzGerald could thus have taken the whole world into his confidence, instead of a few dear friends only, he might have proved a great and moving writer; but he needed the personal relation, the individual tie, to call out his tender, melancholy thought.

It is a task of great difficulty to endeavour to fix the position of FitzGerald with regard to the literary tradition of the age. The truth is that he was essentially an amateur; he was enabled by a curious conjuncture of fortunate circumstances to give to the world one minute piece of absolutely first-rate work. But the *Omar* cannot be said to have affected the stream of English poetry very deeply; it has not turned the current of poetical thought in the direction of Oriental verse; moreover, the language of the *Omar*, stately and beautiful as it is, has no modernity about it; it is not a development, but a reverting to older traditions, a memorable graft, so to speak, of a bygone style.

FitzGerald's position with regard to the poetry that was rising and swelling about him is as that of a stranded boat on a lee-shore. He could not bring himself into line with modern verse at all; he had none of the nineteenth-century spirit. Yet he is in the forefront of those who, standing apart from the direct current of the time, seem destined to make the Victorian age furnish a singularly rich anthology of beautiful poetry. How many poets there are in the last century whose work does not entitle them to be called great poets, who yet have produced a very little of the best quality of poetry. The same is singularly true of the Elizabethan age, which produced not only great poets, but a large number of poetasters whose work rises in a few lyrics into the very front rank.

With FitzGerald it may be plainly said that, with the exception of *Omar* and *The Meadows in Spring*, all the rest of his deliberate work in verse is second-rate, the product of a gifted and accomplished amateur.

But, in prose, there still remain the wonderful letters; and these have a high value, both for their beautiful and original literary form, for the careless picture they give of a certain type of retired and refined country life, for their unconsidered glimpses of great personalities, and for the fact that they present a very peculiar and interesting point of view, a delicate criticism of life from a highly original standpoint. The melancholy which underlies the letters is not a practical or inspiring thing, but it is essentially true; and it carries with it a sad refinement, a temperate waiting upon the issues of life, a sober resignation, which are pure and noble. FitzGerald, by his lover-like tenderness of heart, his wistful desire to clasp hands with life, was enabled to resist the temptation, apt to beset similar temperaments, to sink into a dreary silence about the whole unhappy business. And thus there emerges a certain gentle and pathetic philosophy, not a philosophy for the brisk, the eager, and the successful, but a philosophy for all who find their own defects of character too strong for them, and yet would not willingly

collapse into petulant bitterness.   FitzGerald is a sort
of sedate Hamlet; the madness that wrought in his
brain does not emerge in loud railings, or in tem-
pestuous and brief agonies of desperate action; but it
emerges in many gentle gestures and pathetic beckon-
ings, and a tender desire, in a world where so much is
dark, that men should cling all together and float into
the darkness.   There are many who cannot believe and
cannot act—and for these, as for FitzGerald, it seems
best to hold fast to all that is dear and beautiful.   To
such as these FitzGerald speaks heart to heart; and,
after all, no gifts of style, no brisk technique can ever
take the place of that closeness of fellowship, which
seems to be the only human power that may perhaps
defy even Death.

CHAPTER VII

CRITICISM

FITZGERALD'S letters are full of critical judgments, personal predilections in literature, art, and music, little pronouncements, nice appreciations. He was more of a connoisseur than a critic, a taster of fragrant essences, an inhaler of subtle aromas. But his perception of quality was so innate, and his discriminating attitude so integral a part of his temperament and character, that it is advisable to treat his critical position separately. As a critic, he is remarkable not so much for his largeness and sureness, as for his delicacy and subtlety. His field was limited; the fine fibres of his sympathy could not wholly permeate the mass of literature; affectation, pedantry, mannerisms of certain kinds erected, as it were, a fence about particular authors which he could not penetrate. His reading was in one way wider and in another way narrower than that of most of his contemporaries. He was not so much insular as eclectic; differences of national spirit and an unfamiliar medium of language rather stimulated than hindered his appreciation. What did hamper him were certain almost pettish, childish, feminine prejudices of his own mind and taste. If an author irritated him at the outset, he did not try to understand him; in this respect his judgment was amateurish, like his other work; he was vivid but not broad. His criticism, to use a metaphor, is like a stream, rapid and bright, with deep translucent pools, but without navigable channels. Within certain limits his taste, his *flair* were perfect. He had a pre-eminent sense of quality. He was not imposed upon by volubility or even by daring. In the case of critics less sensitive to quality, volubility is often mistaken for imagination, and daring for strength. But where FitzGerald sympathised, he instinctively divined whether the artist was master of his craft, or whether he was only a little way ahead of his hearers.

The one great quality which seems to have rather escaped FitzGerald was the quality of prodigal vigour. He was a critic rather of detail than of conception. He was fully awake to small, felicitous effects. But he underestimated large authors with definite mannerisms such as Milton, Browning, Victor Hugo, and Thackeray. His criticisms of Shakespeare, for instance, are dictated rather by admiration for his delicacies than by stupefaction at his greatness. The unpardonable sins to FitzGerald were uncouthness and slovenliness.

The same tendency is traceable in his criticism of art, of music, of landscape, even of life. He tended to concentrate himself upon some salient point, some minute effect, rather than upon the general characteristics, the harmony of scene; as he wrote to Crabbe, recalling Cambridge: "Ah, I should like a drive over Newmarket Heath, *the sun shining on the distant leads of Ely Cathedral*"; and to W. F. Pollock, of Oxford: "The façade of Christ Church to the street (by Wren, I believe) is what most delights me; *and the voice of Tom in his Tower.*" His mind and memory worked, so to speak, in vignettes. He remembered the day, the hour, the momentary emotion, rather than the period or the underlying thought.

The nature of FitzGerald's appreciation of beauty
becomes more and more apparent when we consider
his preferences in art and music. In art he was essentially an amateur; he made no comprehensive study of
it. But his dicta on pictures contain many subtle
literary appreciations, enough to show that if he had
taken up art as his life's work he could have been a
very delicate critic. But here again we are met at
every point by prejudices, and by the fact that, with
FitzGerald, a prejudice once conceived was an invincible barrier to further acquaintance; his ingenuity
was all directed, when he had once adopted an attitude
of hostility, to finding arguments to support his view.
He had no idea of conquering prejudices, or of trying
to see into the strength of a painter and the motives
which guided him.

He had, moreover, a strong belief in his own canons
of criticism. He wrote to Samuel Laurence, in the first
letter he ever addressed to him : " I suppose a visit to
Rome, or an exact technical knowledge of pictures, is
very essential. I am sure I can understand the finest
part of pictures without doing either."

There was nothing progressive in FitzGerald's love
of art; he was content to stand in the ancient ways,
and only too much inclined to dislike, in a perverse
way, all signs of modern development. Just as he
disliked the Pre-Raphaelite school of poetry, he disliked the Pre-Raphaelite conception of painting.

What he demanded in art was the wholesome, simple
established mode of conception and execution. He
could not put himself in a new posture, or sympathise
with a revolutionary tendency.

The same is the case with his appreciation of
music, which moved him profoundly. He desired
tranquil beauty, tenderness, simplicity; he hated all

tricks, all straining after effects, all melodramatic complications.

Thus he wrote :—

"I grow every day more and more to love only the old God save the King style : the common chords, those truisms of music, like other truisms so little understood in the full. Just look at the mechanism of Robin Adair."

All his delight was in pure, simple, massive music : he loved the old English composers.

"We [Crabbe's son and daughter] with not a voice among us, go through Handel's Coronation Anthem ! Laughable it may seem ; yet it is not quite so ; the things are so well defined, simple, and grand, that the faintest outline of them tells, my admiration of the old Giant grows and grows ; his is the music for a great, active people ! "

We see then that both in painting and in music FitzGerald was on the look-out for purity and simplicity of effect. But one feels that in his artistic and musical criticisms he was only chronicling personal predilections and preferences ; he gave no reasons for the faith that was in him. He could never disconnect art from life ; and thus the art which could touch the emotions of simple people and play a part in common life, by stirring the tranquil sense of beauty in normal minds, seemed to him a greater and more desirable thing than the art of those in search of remote, mystical, and incommunicable ideals.

Here again he was dominated by the simple commonsense which was so strongly marked a characteristic of his whole nature, and which makes him on the whole so just and sane a critic. But just for this very reason he had no catholicity of taste ; he could not sympathise with the difficult raptures, the transcendent realism which raises art higher from platform to platform. The dimly apprehended secrets, the thrilling of sacred emotions, the pontifical responsibilities which work so strongly in the most sensitive and esoteric natures were a closed book to FitzGerald. These would have seemed to him mere pretentious phantoms, an unreal and hectic posturing, an attempt to disguise an egotistic discontent under an affected solemnity.

In literary regions, FitzGerald had a considerable confidence in his own critical judgment. He wrote to Cowell :—

" . . . You, I, and John Allen are among the few, I do say, who, having a good natural Insight, maintain it undimmed by public, or private, Regards."

And again, to the same, in a sentence which commemorates the extinction of FitzGerald's faint ambitions to be an original writer, and his demure acceptance of the critical attitude :—

"Ten years ago I might have been vext to see you striding along in Sanscrit and Persian so fast ; reading so much ; remembering all ; writing about it so well. But now I am glad to see any man do any thing well ; and I know that it is my vocation to stand and wait, and know within myself whether it *is* done well."

And late in life to Lowell :—

" I am accredited with the Aphorism, 'Taste is the Feminine of Genius.' However that may be, I have some confidence in my own."

He gives an account of the spirit in which he read, in early days, which shows that he demanded to appreciate rather than to master the spirit of a writer :—

" I take pleasure in reading things I don't wholly understand ; just as the old women like sermons ; I think it is of a piece with an admiration of all Nature around us. I think there is a greater charm in the half meanings and glimpses of

meaning that come in through Blake's wilder visions : though
his difficulties arose from a very different source from Shakespeare's. But somewhat too much of this. I suspect I have
found out this as an useful solution, when I am asked the
meaning of anything that I am admiring, and don't know it."

But, as has been said, FitzGerald was always a critic
of detail and form, rather than a critic of tendencies
and currents in literature. It will therefore be convenient to give some of his more detailed views, for it
is in these rather than in general judgments that his
strength lay. He had in the first place a great devotion
to the Greek and Latin Classics. We find him reading Homer, Æschylus, Thucydides, Plutarch, Pindar,
Xenophon, Menander, and Herodotus. On several of
these authors he made characteristic comments. He
thought Plutarch, he says, " such a gentleman." He
took up Thucydides, and soon found himself reading it
"like a novel." But of all Classical authors he put
Sophocles far the first, reading him repeatedly.
Euripides he tried, but found his subtlety and *doctrin-
aire* morality intolerable. For Homer's *Iliad*, " with
its brutal Gods and Heroes," he could not care. Of
Æschylus and Sophocles he writes :—

" Sophocles is a pure Greek temple ; but Æschylus is a
rugged mountain, lashed by seas, and riven by thunderbolts :
and which is the most wonderful, and appalling ? Or if one
will have Æschylus too a work of man, I say he is like a
Gothic Cathedral, which the Germans say did arise from the
genius of man aspiring up to the immeasurable, and reaching
after the infinite in complexity and gloom, according as
Christianity elevated and widened men's minds. . . . Besides
these Æschyluses *trouble* us with their grandeur and gloom ;
but Sophocles is always soothing, complete, and satisfactory."

In this connection it is interesting to note that he
often implored Tennyson to translate a play of

Sophocles. "Every great poet," he used to say, "owes this as a duty to his predecessors."

In Latin he read Tacitus, Juvenal, Lucretius, Seneca, and most of all Virgil, who made his eyes wet, as he says, and whom he loved. Horace he never really cared for. "Why is it," he wrote, "that I can never take up with Horace—so sensible, agreeable, elegant, and sometimes even grand ?"

Even with an author like Virgil, whom he devotedly loved, he can lay his finger on the one defect, namely, the disproportion of ornament to conception of subject. But it is clear from his preference of Virgil to Catullus, that he was always inclined to value tenderness more highly than passion.

"I have also been visiting dear old Virgil : his *Georgics* and the sixth and eighth books of the *Æneid*. I could now take them up and read them both again. Pray look at lines 407-415 of Book viii.—the poor Matron kindling her early fire —so Georgic! so Virgilian ! so unsuited, or disproportionate, to the Thing it illustrates."

Of Lucretius he wrote :—

" . . . I have been regaling myself, in my unscholarly way, with Mr. Munro's admirable *Lucretius* . . . I venerate the earnestness of the man, and the power with which he makes some music even from his hardest Atoms. . . . I forget if Lucretius is in Dante ; he should have been the Guide thro' Hell ; but perhaps he was too deep in it to get out for a Holiday."

And the following extract on Seneca is full of originality :—

"I wonder whether old Seneca was indeed such a humbug as people now say he was : he is really a fine writer. About three hundred years ago, or less, our divines and writers called him the divine Seneca ; and old Bacon is full of him. One sees in him the upshot of all the Greek philosophy, how it stood in Nero's time, when the Gods had worn out a great deal. I don't think old Seneca believed he should live again. Death is his great resource. Think of the *rococo city* of a gentleman studying Seneca in the middle of February 1844 in a remarkably damp cottage."

In English FitzGerald read, especially in his first youth, the early balladists and lyrists. He speaks of H. Vaughan, Wotton, Carew, Lily, with high praise— "very English and very pleasant."

In poetry generally he was hard to please; he revelled in Shakespeare, both sonnets and plays, but he disliked Milton and Spenser; he admired Dryden, especially as a prose writer; Cowper and Pope he called men of genius, but out of his sphere. Gray he ranked very high. Wordsworth he loved, but he seldom mentions him without some touch of irritation at his pomposity. Of moderns the three Tennysons, Alfred, Frederic, and Charles; but of most contemporary poetry he spoke in terms of great contempt; he said, for instance, of a poetical friend, "He talks of publishing a popular edition of his poems: he means a cheap one."

In English prose he read at one time a good deal of the older divines, Barrow, Jeremy Taylor, South, and Warburton. He admired Burton's *Anatomy of Melancholy*; he loved both Fielding and Richardson, preferring the latter. He called *Clarissa Harlowe* "wonderful and aggravating" and often desired to make an abbreviation of it. He admired Burke. He was fond of the *Spectator*, and thought at one time of making a little book out of the Roger de Coverley essays. It is surprising from all points of view that he did not care for Jane Austen. He loved an old book like Harrington's *Oceana*, the kind of large, quiet book that you find in an old country-house. He was fond of big, leisurely biographies such as Boswell's *Johnson* and the *Life and Journals of John Wesley.* He enjoyed Horace Walpole's and Cowper's letters and admired Sheridan. He read a little of philosophy, such as Spinoza, but his mind turned more to the definite and personal; he said once that he wished we had more diaries of unknown men.

Of purely modern literature he read little. He was very fond of Newman, both the *Apologia* and the *Sermons.* He read the *Life of Arnold* with interest. Of modern novels he read both Dickens and Thackeray with critical admiration; and he was fond both of Wilkie Collins and Trollope; but he never appreciated George Eliot. Indeed he loved romances rather than novels. He was fond of reading George Borrow, but complained of his lapses into vulgarities of expression. He read Emerson, but found him misty and intangible; he thought Hawthorne a genius, but "not altogether to his taste." Carlyle he criticised harshly enough in early days. "Carlyle raves and foams, but he has nothing to propose"; but after making his acquaintance he began to feel differently. "There is a bottom of truth in his wildest rhapsodies," he wrote.

It speaks well for FitzGerald's critical acumen that he discovered Blake for himself in 1833 and wrote of him with bewildered admiration.

As to his Oriental studies, there is a recorded comment which casts a curious light upon his taste for them. "When I look into Homer, Dante, Virgil, Æschylus, Shakespeare," he said, "those Orientals look silly."

I have thought it well to collect these scattered preferences, because they illustrate the nature of Fitz-Gerald's critical judgment. It will be seen that it is essentially whimsical; he touched literature at

many points, but there is no catholicity of view. He
is like a man walking in a garden of flowers, attracted
here by a perfume, there by a colour, and, with an
almost childlike pettishness, refusing to look at anything except what happens to strike his fastidious
perception. His individuality is his only guide.

The charm of his literary criticisms is that they
come out so simply, in a kind of fireside ease, from a
man who has read books because he loved them, without any pontifical solemnity—and yet they are as true
and penetrating as those of Charles Lamb himself: he
began to criticise early. He writes in 1832 :—

" . . . Shakespeare's (sonnets) are perfectly simple, and
have the very essence of tenderness . . . they seem all stuck
about my heart, like the ballads that used to be on the walls
of London."

He could never bring himself really to care for
Milton ; he wrote :—

"Then Milton ; I don't think I've read him these forty
years ; the whole Scheme of the Poem, and certain Parts of
it, looming as grand as anything in my Memory ; but I never
could read ten lines together without stumbling at some
Pedantry that tipped me at once out of Paradise, or even
Hell, into the Schoolroom, worse than either. Tennyson
again used to say that the two grandest of all Similes were
those of the Ships hanging in the Air, and 'the Gunpowder
one,' which he used slowly and grimly to enact, in the Days
that are no more. He certainly then thought Milton the
sublimest of all the Gang ; his Diction modelled on Virgil,
as perhaps Dante's."

The following is an interesting apppreciation of
Dryden's prose, written to Lowell :—

" As in the case of your Essays, I don't pretend to say
which is finest : but I think that to me Dryden's Prose, *quoad*
Prose, is the finest Style of all. So Gray, I believe, thought :

that man of Taste, very far removed, perhaps as far as feminine from masculine, from the Man he admired."

What could be more penetrating than the following criticism of Walpole's letters, written, it must be remembered, to a girl :—

" . . . You spoke once of even trying Walpole's Letters : capital as they are to me, I can't be sure they would much interest, even if they did not rather disgust, you : the Man and his Times are such as you might not care for at all, though there are such men as his, and such Times too, in the world. . . . *N.B.*—It is not gross or coarse : but you would not like the man, so satirical, selfish, and frivolous, you would think.   But I think I could show you that he had a very loving Heart for a few, and a very firm, just, understanding under all his Wit and Fun.   Even Carlyle has admitted that he was about the clearest-sighted Man of his time."

His criticisms of Gray are very delicate :—

" As to Gray—Ah, to think of that little Elegy inscribed among the Stars, while ——, —— and Co. are blazing away with their Fireworks here below.   I always think that there is more Genius in most of the three volume Novels than in Gray: but by the most exquisite Taste, and indefatigable lubrication, he made of his own few thoughts, and many of other men's, a something which we all love to keep ever about us.   I do not think his scarcity of work was from Design : he had but a little to say, I believe, and took his time to say it. . . ."

Keats he greatly admired ; he wrote to Mrs. Kemble :—

" Talking of Keats, do not forget to read Lord Houghton's Life and Letters of him : in which you will find what you may not have guessed from his Poetry (though almost unfathomably deep in that also), the strong, masculine, Sense and Humour, etc., of the man : more akin to Shakespeare, I am tempted to think, in a perfect circle of Poetic Faculties, than any Poet since."

A figure in English literature for whom FitzGerald

had a special tenderness and sympathy was Charles
Lamb; he wrote:—

"We have also Memoirs of Godwin, very dry, I think;
indeed with very little worth reading, except two or three
Letters of dear Charles Lamb, 'Saint Charles,' as Thackeray
once called him, while looking at one of his half-mad Letters,
and remember[ing] his Devotion to that quite mad Sister. I
must say I think his Letters infinitely better than his Essays;
and Patmore[1] says his conversation, when just enough animated
by Gin and Water, was better than either, which I believe
too. Procter said he was far beyond the Coleridges, Words-
worths, Southeys, etc. And I am afraid I believe that also."

FitzGerald grew to love Charles Lamb more and
more as life went on, just as he grew to love Wordsworth less.

The following is a youthful criticism in the earlier
and more deliberate manner, with the slightest
possible affectation of simplicity; but none the less
perspicacious:—

"I have been poring over Wordsworth lately: which has
had much effect in bettering my Blue Devils: for his philosophy does not abjure melancholy, but puts a pleasant counten-
ance upon it, and connects it with humanity. It is very well,
if the sensibility that makes us fearful of ourselves is diverted
to become a cause of sympathy and interest with Nature and
mankind: and this I think Wordsworth tends to do."

Later on FitzGerald's view of Wordsworth was
much modified. He never ceased to admire the sober
majesty, the grave tranquillity of the best work; but
the more he knew of the man and his nature, the more
was he irritated and perplexed by the affectation, the
deliberate solemnity, the pose of the poet who had set
out in quest of directness and simplicity. The truth
which perhaps FitzGerald did not quite comprehend, is

[1] Peter George Patmore (1786-1855), father of the poet
Coventry Patmore.

that Wordsworth was not only a man and a poet; the instinct of the teacher lay in the very marrow of his bones; and in proportion as the impulse of the poet died away, the impulse of the teacher emerged. Wordsworth fell into the lamentable error, characteristic of earnest-minded men without humour, of taking himself too seriously and overestimating the value of his own influence. FitzGerald felt the poet's attitude to be both pretentious and grotesque; and therefore, though he could not help venerating him, it delighted him to poke fun at the rather self-conscious prophet.

FitzGerald worshipped Scott, read and re-read him in the days of strong sight; and in the days of clouded vision had the novels read to him. Scott opened a door to him into an enchanted world, not the dreary, familiar world he knew so well and was often so wearied of, but into a brave, bright country of fair ladies and shrewd crones, of freebooters and knights and gallant gentlemen. As life went on and Fitz-Gerald grew old he used to say that the thought, that the particular novel of Scott's which was being read to him he might never hear again, threw a little cloud of sadness over his mind. Scott's defects as a writer seemed to FitzGerald to float like straws on a river deep and wide.

He wrote to W. F. Pollock :—

" . . . The *Pirate* is, I know, not one of Scott's best: the Women, Minna, Brenda, Norna, are poor theatrical figures. But Magnus and Jack Bunce and Claud Halcro (though the latter rather wearisome) are substantial enough: how wholesomely they swear! and no one ever thinks of blaming Scott for it. There is a passage where the Company at Burgh Westra are summoned by Magnus to go down to the Shore to see the Boats go off to the Deep Sea fishing, and 'they followed his stately step to the Shore as the Herd of Deer

follows the leading Stag, with all manner of respectful
Observance.' This, coming in at the close of the preceding
unaffected Narrative, is to me like Homer, whom Scott really
resembles in the simplicity and ease of his Story. . . . I
finished the Book with Sadness; thinking I might never read
it again. . . ."

In 1874, though by that time averse to leaving
home, he paid a pious pilgrimage to Abbotsford. The
following is his account of it :—

"But I did get to Abbotsford, and was rejoiced to find it
was not at all Cockney, not a Castle, but only in the half-
castellated style of heaps of other houses in Scotland ; the
Grounds simply and broadly laid out before the windows,
down to a field, down to the Tweed, with the woods which he
left so little, now well aloft and flourishing, and I was glad.
I could not find my way to Maida's Grave in the Garden,
with its false quantity,

                "' Ad jānuam Domini, etc.,'
which the Whigs and Critics taunted Scott with, and Lockhart had done it. 'You know I don't care a curse about what
I write'; nor about what was imputed to him. In this,
surely like Shakespeare : as also in other respects. I will
worship him, in spite of Gurlyle, who sent me an ugly
Autotype of Knox whom I was to worship instead.

"Then I went to see Jedburgh[1] Abbey, in a half-ruined
corner of which he lies entombed—Lockhart beside him—a
beautiful place, with his own Tweed still running close by, and
his Eildon Hills looking on. The man who drove me about
showed me a hill which Sir Walter was very fond of visiting,
from which he could see over the Border, etc. This hill is between Abbotsford and Jedburgh[1] : and when his Coach horses,
who drew his Hearse, got there, to that hill, they could scarce
be got on."

The last touch, the pathos of the incident, is just the
sort of thing that went straight to FitzGerald's heart.
He could not forbear to give Carlyle an account of the

---

[1] A slip for Dryburgh.

pilgrimage, adding : "Oh, I know you think Scott a
brave, honest, good-natured man, and a good Story-
teller, only not a Hero at all.   And I can't help knowing and loving him as such."

Dickens, too, held a high place in FitzGerald's heart.
He felt very strongly the vital force of Dickens as a
creator, the way in which, as by the waving of a wand,
he could make an incident live and breathe.

Thus he wrote : —

"The intended Pathos is, as usual, missed : but just turn to
Little Dombey's Funeral, where the Acrobat in the Street
suspends his performance till the Funeral has passed, and his
Wife wonders if the little Acrobat in her Arms will so far out-
live the little boy in the Hearse as to wear a Ribbon through
his hair, following his Father's Calling.   It is in such Side-
touches, you know, that Dickens is inspired to Create like a
little God Almighty."

He hardly knew Dickens personally ; but it was a
great joy to him to read Forster's *Life*, and to find not
only a magician and a story-teller, but a man, who,
whatever were his faults, was full to the brim of
generosity and human affection.

For Browning he had the most limited sympathy.
His dislike of the coarseness of workmanship, the
deliberate grotesqueness of phrase, the tendency to
kick up the heels and gambol about in sheer zest of
living, blinded FitzGerald, one must suppose, to the
tenderness, the amazing range of the man's humanity.
He wrote to Frederic Tennyson :—

"I see your old friend Browning is in the field again, with
another of his odd titles : De Saisiez—or Croisic—or some
such name.   I tried to read his Dramatic Lyrics again : they
seemed to me Ingoldsby Legends."

In Italian he read and loved Dante and Boccaccio ;
but could not care for Tasso or Ariosto.   In Spanish,

though he spent so much time and pains over Calderon,
yet he put *Don Quixote* almost at the head of all his
books, loving, as he said, even the Dictionary in which
he looked out the words.

In French he often read Montaigne, and almost
adored Madame de Sévigné's letters. He took pleasure in Béranger, and in Sainte-Beuve; Victor Hugo
he did not care for, or the Romantic school generally.

He was never really in sympathy with French
literature; he desired above all things simplicity,
directness, homeliness on the one hand, and sublimity,
grandeur, largeness on the other. But all finesse,
affectation, prettiness and elegant trifling was against
his taste.

Thus he wrote, comparing ancient and modern
French poetry :—

"I never understand why the old French Poetry is to my
Palate, while the modern is not. Partly, no doubt, because
of his *naïveté*, which is lost from educated Frenchmen."

And his deliberate judgments on French literature are
prejudiced by the same feeling :—

"So it is with nearly all French things ; there is a clever,
showy surface ; but no Holy of Holies far withdrawn ; conceived in the depth of a mind, and only to be received into
the depth of ours after much attention."

And of *Gil Blas* :—

"I have failed in another attempt at *Gil Blas*. I believe
I see its easy Grace, humour, etc. But it is (like La Fontaine)
too thin a Wine for me : all sparkling with little adventures,
but no one to care about ; no Colour, no Breadth, like my
dear Don ; whom I shall resort to forthwith."

With Germany and German literature he had no
sympathy at all. He profoundly disliked the tendency
to æsthetic philosophising, and awkward gush which
he believed to characterise the Teutonic spirit :—

"Then there's an account of Hallam's Literature, with a deal about *Æsthetics* in it.   Oh Pollock! let you and I and Spedding stand out against these damnable German humbugs."

From the above it is easy to deduce FitzGerald's literary taste. He was indolent and eclectic; he can hardly be called a very wide reader; he was not like Macaulay, an omnivorous gorger upon books; such an appetite indeed as Macaulay indulged in reading is of the nature of intellectual gluttony. It is a symptom of a restlessness of brain, and reading becomes a mere habit, a kind of mental sedative like smoking or card-playing, or the occupations with which men of active minds ward off the approaches of ennui. FitzGerald had none of this kind of restlessness; he was essentially a spectatorial and meditative man; his reading was not merely to satiate a craving, but a contemplative process; with his deficiency of intellectual initia-tive, he used the authors whom he read somewhat like beaters, to start game in the coverts of his own mind; he did not devour, he sipped and tasted, the book serving often as a mere text which gave his own languid fancy material for dreams; he was not an absorbed reader, but a leisurely one; mind and eye alike would desert the page, and the dream-pictures would come crowding before the inner sense. The omnivorous reader wins delight from throwing himself into the author's mind; he is like a man who wanders in a strange house alone, paces the galleries as in the palace of art, feeds upon what he sees without ques-tioning or analysing. But it was far otherwise with FitzGerald. He was by instinct a connoisseur; he ap-praised, distinguished, weighed. He liked to stand by, as he said, and know within himself whether the thing was well done, as a man might stand to watch a game.

Then, too, his taste was all for the detailed, the personal, the precise. He loved the stuff out of which life is made, the pathos, the humour, the beauty and sorrow of the world. There are very few allusions to history or to current politics in his letters; there is a kind of lofty and emotional patriotism, a tender love for the land he lived in; but here again he grew with advancing years, like most shy, inactive men, a pessimist; he thought with sorrow that England was coarsening and growing debilitated; and this because he was not himself in the forefront of the battle, and because such generous ideals as he had nursed in his youth were growing faded, giving place in the ardent minds of the rising generation to other ideals, not less generous, but which to FitzGerald were simply unfamiliar.

The same process took place in his literary taste; he acted on the principle which Charles Lamb enunciated, that whenever a new book came out he read an old one. There was nothing progressive about Fitz-Gerald's taste; he thought and wrote contemptuously of modern books. He had not the energy to follow the new movements; his sun set early; and the latter part of his life was lived in a remembered light. And to such an extent did his feeling of personality affect his critical judgment that it was said of him humorously that he never really approved of his friends' writings unless he had seen them in manuscript.

But with all his limitations, and they were many and obvious, it still remains true of FitzGerald that he was one of those, who are even fewer than we are apt to think, who have loved high literature with a real instinctive and passionate joy. Even men whose delight in literature is true and deep are apt to find these masterpieces austere and even dreary, to breathe

with difficulty in the serene air. Many of us who
love great literature can only take it in small doses—
otherwise it becomes ineffective and unmeaning, like a
liturgical passage where familiarity veils the beauty,
which yet in a moment of insight flashes upon us in all
its primal awe. But FitzGerald could drink, day after
day, deep draughts from the pure fount, and never
slake his thirst.

His selection of Sophocles as probably the most
perfect of writers is characteristic of him. FitzGerald
was in complete harmony with that gracious and
untroubled spirit—

"εὔκολος μὲν ἔνθαδ', εὔκολος δ' ἐκεῖ,"

who loved life and beauty, and yet stood apart, un-
touched by the fever and the dust of life, watching
humanity from some serener place, lovingly and
generously, but yet remotely, as a man may look
down into the streets from some high tower, and see
the house-roofs and the gardens, and with a kind of
pity the busy little figures hurrying to and fro.

FitzGerald indeed did not attain to that tranquil
standpoint; he was too deeply concerned, and depended
too much on others for that. He hungered and
thirsted for love; and for the sweetness which evaded
his grasp. Yet in his patience, his dignity, his unworldliness, his clear eye for beauty, he had much in
common with the serene tragedian who could look so
unflinchingly into the darkest places of the human
soul and present, as in the *Œdipus*, the spectacle of
one, involved in the most poignant miseries that can
befall a man, deprived of all that can make life
tolerable, yet in that grim descent, surrounded
by all the most hideous and shapeless forms of woe
unutterable, never losing an indomitable dignity of

soul. It was to that dignity that FitzGerald clung
with all his might; and although in his sheltered and
uneventful life there was little room for tragedy on
an august scale, yet he faced the sorrow which lies
plentifully in wait for the sensitive spirit with a
quietude that was philosophical though never stoical.

FitzGerald never fell into the error so natural to
secluded men of taste, of mistaking literature and art,
the reflections of life, for life itself. He did not, like
the Lady of Shalott, live in a self-made paradise; he
was for ever on the road, mixing in his shy way with
mankind; and it is this which makes his letters, and
his Omar—which are the abiding fruit of his genius—
so great, because they never lost hold of realities,
because he worked in the spirit of nature with the
invisible hand of art.   Intellect with FitzGerald
always served emotion. He felt first what he afterwards expressed; the emotion never lagged behind
the expression; and it is that, after all, which differentiates artists, and makes them worthy to move in
the procession,

            " Where none is first or last."

CHAPTER VIII

HABITS—CHARACTER

FitzGerald's habits were absolutely simple; his only plan of action was to do what he liked, and not be bothered. In earlier years he had rambled further afield; but in the quiet days at Woodbridge or Lowestoft, he would spend the morning over books and papers, or write a leisurely letter; he would stroll about, looking at flowers and trees, listening to the voices of birds, talking to his simple acquaintances. Sometimes he would go out in his boat, and gossip with the boatmen. He seems to have had no fixed times for work, but took it up when it pleased his fancy. His books lay all about him in confusion; he had not a large library—some thousand volumes—and he was fond of pulling out leaves which he thought otiose. Sometimes, if the fancy took him, he would call on a neighbour; when he came home in the after-noon he would play his organ or sing to himself. Then he would go to his books again, and, before his eye-sight failed, would read or write; smoke a pipe, and go to bed. All definite engagements he abhorred; he had the nervous and irritable temperament that finds the chatter of irresponsible people distracting and annoying; as he wrote to Mrs. Cowell :—

"I was all yesterday taking a small Party on the River, and am to-day about to do the same. These little things tire me more than you would think possible : really, I believe, from the talking and hearing talk all day, which is so unlike my way of Life. But I am too selfish already in keeping my little Ship to myself."

In the early days of FitzGerald's eremitical life he made experiments in diet, and gradually settled down into vegetarianism. He felt at first a loss of physical power, but this passed off, and he believed he gained in lightness of spirit. He lived practically on bread and fruit, mostly apples and pears—even a turnip—with sometimes cheese, or butter, and milk puddings. But he was not a bigoted vegetarian. To avoid an appearance of singularity he would eat meat at other houses, and provided it in plenty for his guests. But the only social meal he cared to join in was "tea, pure and simple, with bread and butter." He was abstemious, but not a teetotaller; and was a moderate smoker, using clean clay pipes, which he broke in pieces when he had smoked them once. Like all solitary men, he got more and more attached to his own habits, and it became every year more difficult for him to conform to any other mode of life.

We have a curious account from one of his boy-readers of the way in which FitzGerald, in the days of weak sight, spent his evenings. The boy was engaged to read for two hours, from 7.30 to 9.30. This particular reader was so punctual that FitzGerald used to call him "the ghost," because he could be depended upon to make a silent and precise entrance exactly when he was expected. Magazines and current journals were read first; at the time of the Tichborne Trial, for instance, the proceedings of each day were gone through in detail. Then followed a simple supper. Then a novel, or some book like Boswell's *Johnson* or Pepys' *Diary* would be embarked upon. FitzGerald's temper was a little uncertain. He would apply hard words to both reader and author. If he was bored, he would fidget and say, "Oh, pass that d——d rot!" If he was unusually hard on the reader, he would apologise afterwards or even proffer a small tip, which he called "insulting the boy in a pecuniary manner."

FitzGerald himself sat on a low chair with his feet on the fender, in dressing-gown and slippers. He invariably wore his tall hat, only removing it occasionally to get a red silk handkerchief out of it. He would hold his snuff-box in his hand, or a paper-knife; if he was interested he would sit silent, stroking his beard with the paper-knife; if he was not interested he would make endless interruptions.

FitzGerald's pleasures and preferences were of the simplest kind. He had an almost childish delight in bright colours, a thing which is said to be rare in light-eyed men. His favourite flowers were the nasturtium, the geranium, the convolvulus—"the morning glory"—with its purple or white trumpets, the marigold, not only for its bold hues, but for its courage in living the winter through. He loved the garish tints of bright curtains and carpets, the plumage of gay birds, cocks and pheasants, the splendours of butterflies and moths, anything that could warm and invigorate the eye and heart.

Thus he speaks of looking from the river on the crops, "as they grow green, yellow, russet, and are finally carried away in the red and blue waggons with the sorrel horse." A parti-coloured mop that he had bought for household purposes was so pleasing a fount of colour that it stood for years in his room. He had the same delight in sweet, cheerful, and tunable sounds. He liked the crowing of cocks, the notes of brisk birds. Of the blackbird he said that its song "seemed so jolly and the note so proper from that golden bill of his." The nightingale he cared for less, saying whimsically that at the time she chose to discourse she "ought to be in bed like the rest of us." He liked the sound of bells, the wind in the trees, the rattle of ropes, the sharp hiss of moving seas. In all of these things he had the perception of quality, of essence, of individuality clearly defined.

FitzGerald was photographed in 1873, when he was nearly sixty-four, by Messrs. Cade and White of Ipswich. He named one of the two portraits taken, the "philosopher" portrait, and the other the "statesman" portrait. In both, the high domed forehead is quite bald, and the hair grows long and limp over his collar. He has thin whiskers. Both the pictures have an expression of fatigue. The "philosopher's" eyes are cast down; but in the "statesman" portrait they are upturned, and have a dim, sunken look; the eyelids are half-shut, testifying to weakness of sight. The cheeks are somewhat hollow; the nose finely cut and inclined to aquiline; the broad, mobile mouth, with its big lips, is much depressed at the corners, giving the face a wistful and regretful look. There is a strongly marked dimple in the chin. It is a somewhat indolent face, and has an expression of vague trouble—not the face of a successful or even of a contented man. Some allowance must no doubt be made for the fact that to be photographed was obviously a trying ordeal to FitzGerald; but a life-history is written legibly upon it. We can see the dreamer of dreams, the sad dignity of one who saw clearly and without illusion the dark background of life. It is the face of one with great intellectual power, but dogged by a deep-seated irresolution and conscious of a certain failure of aim. But it has too a very sweet and tender look, the look of one who has loved much, and whom suffering has not made either cold or hard, though he has found the world too strong.

Such was FitzGerald near at hand. To those who saw him abroad, he appeared a tall, dreamy-looking man, blue-eyed, with large, sensitive lips, and a melancholy expression; his face tanned with exposure to the sun; moving his head as he walked with a remote, almost a haughty air, as though he guarded his own secret; strong and active from much exercise, yet irresolute in his movements; with straggling grey hair, and slovenly in dress, wearing an ancient, battered, black-banded, shiny-edged, tall hat, round which he would in windy weather tie a handk'erchief to keep it in its place; his clothes of baggy blue cloth, as though he were a seafarer, his trousers short and his shoes low, exhibiting a length of white or grey stockings. With an unstarched white shirt-front, high, crumpled, stand-up collars, a big, black silk tie in a careless bow; in cold weather trailing a green and black or grey plaid shawl; in hot weather even walking barefoot, with his boots slung to a stick. He never carried an umbrella except in the heaviest rain. Such was the inconsequent appearance presented by FitzGerald at the age of sixty. But it must be remembered that this costume was not so strange in the sixties as it would be at the present day. Indeed, its strangeness then principally consisted in the fact that it was an unusual combination of formality and informality.

Everything about him bore the mark of strong unconventionality; and it is strange how men who love their own ways, and desire to live in the world rather as ghosts than men, so often fail to understand that conformity to conventional usage is often the best and safest disguise.

But FitzGerald had a radical abhorrence of conventional things; he was impatient of the least hint of tyranny; it was characteristic of him that on returning from a cruise in the Deben, he could not wait till the boat drew to land, but would generally step out in the shallow water, wetting himself to the knees. There ran indeed through all his habits a certain want of self-control that is of the nature of madness—the madness that he so often claimed as the inheritance of his family—a species of childish surrender to the whim of the moment, an absence of self-command.

His relations with other people are characterised by the same whimsical self-will. FitzGerald had an extraordinary fund of sentiment in his nature; "his friendships," as he said of himself, "were more like loves." He was not only affectionate, he was deeply and devotedly loyal to his friends. Though he lost sight, to a great extent, of the comrades of his youth, because he could not bring himself to be a guest in any house where he was not absolutely unmolested and able to follow his own whims, yet he managed by his letters to keep the bond drawn close. Both Thackeray and Tennyson declared that they loved FitzGerald best of all their friends; even Carlyle, with all his enthusiasm for action, kept a very warm corner in his heart for FitzGerald. But this sentiment had in FitzGerald's case a weaker side. He was always taking fancies, and once under the spell, he could see no faults in his friend. His friendship for Browne rose out of one of these romantic impulses; so too his affection for Posh, the boatman; for Cowell, and for Alfred Smith the farmer of Farlingay and Boulge, who had been his protégé as a boy. He seems, too, to have been one of those whose best friendships are reserved for men; for though he had beloved women friends like Mrs. Cowell

and Mrs. Kemble, yet these are the exceptions rather
than the rule. The truth is that there was a strong
admixture of the feminine in FitzGerald's character.
As a rule the friendships of men are equal, unromantic
comradeships, which take no account of such physical
things as face and gesture and voice. But FitzGerald
had again an almost feminine observation of personal
characteristics. Browne's wholesome, manly beauty,
the comeliness of Alfred Smith, the strength and
vigour of Posh, the splendid majesty of Tennyson, the
sweet-tempered smile of Cowell—all these played their
part in determining the devotion of FitzGerald.

But even so his relations to his friends had the less
attractive elements, such as the contradictory pettishness which he lavished on Browne, the disagreeable
and cutting things which he said to him, to be followed
by a tearful repentance; the curious sense of irritable
dignity which used to transpose him in a moment into
a formidable and fastidious gentleman—all these are
referable to the same feminine characteristics, the
desire to dominate a situation, to show a momentary
power at whatever cost. He could be perfectly easy
and familiar with unaffected people; he could sit,
chat, smoke, take his meals with boatmen, farmers,
and tradespeople. But he was thoroughly uncertain
and capricious in his behaviour. He could thank a
stranger with almost exaggerated gratitude for a little
service done him, and he could at the same time say to
a Woodbridge neighbour who greeted him with a
genial Good-morning, "I don't know you!" because
they had never been formally introduced. When the
rector of Woodbridge visited him and said, "I am
sorry, Mr. FitzGerald, that I never see you at church,"
he could reply with Johnsonian rotundity, "Sir, you
might have conceived that a man has not come to my

years without thinking much on those things. I believe
I may say that I have reflected on them fully. You
need not repeat this visit." Again, he could torment
even his beloved sailor-folk in the same way. John
Green of Aldeburgh, a boatman, said that on one
occasion he had showed himself very attentive to
FitzGerald, doing this and that without orders.
"I suppose you think you've got the Prince of Wales
here," said FitzGerald. The next time that they were
together, Green held back. "I suppose I'm not worth
waiting on," said FitzGerald.

Though much annoyed by any discourtesy shown
him by others, he was by no means invariably courteous himself. He invited a bookseller, Mr. Read of
Woodbridge, whose shop he often visited, to dinner
on one occasion. Mr. Read appeared at the appointed
time, and was sturdily refused admittance. He re-
monstrated in vain, and finally returned home in
considerable vexation. On the following day he
received a note from FitzGerald which did not mend
matters. "I saw you yesterday when you called,"
FitzGerald wrote, "but I was not fit for company,
and felt that I could not be bothered."

He was capable of administering a humorous rebuke,
if necessary. On one occasion, in early life, he was
present at a gathering of friends; one of the company,
who was fond of titled society, aired his acquaintance
with people of importance, and told pointless anecdotes
of distinguished friends. FitzGerald listened with an
appearance of deep melancholy, and finally rose to his
feet; he lighted a bedroom candle, and at the door,
standing candle in hand, with a look of hopeless dejection, said, "I once knew a lord too, but he is dead."

For all his philosophy, he was very quick to resent
the smallest familiarity which he felt to be undue;

indeed a fondness for making people uncomfortable is characteristic of rather childish natures, who above all things desire to make themselves felt.

He was always impatient of being interfered with when his thoughts were occupied; one evening when his boy was reading to him, FitzGerald pottered about, turning over books and papers, searching for something. The boy offered his help to look for the missing object; FitzGerald refused the proffered assistance, adding pettishly, "That is just about the way I shall get to heaven, I suppose, searching for what I cannot find."

When he was walking along the road or the street with a companion he would get so much absorbed in his own thoughts that if he was addressed he would answer in a querulous voice as though annoyed by impertinent interruptions. His husky voice, with a curious deflection of tone at the end of his sentences, was highly characteristic. "He used to speak," said Mowbray Donne, "like a cricket ball with a break in it," or "like a wave falling over—a Suffolk wave." This inaccessibility, accompanied by a good deal of *hauteur* of manner, was even displayed to his nearest friends. Miss Crabbe said of him that he was a distant and punctilious man; "I think," she said, "we all stood in awe of him, and my impression was that he was a proud man; and, like many proud people, didn't mind at all doing things that many people wouldn't do, such as carrying his boots to be mended." She adds that he never seemed light-hearted, but always oppressed with a kind of brooding melancholy.

Though self-indulgent himself in many ways, he disliked any apparent grossness of enjoyment in others. "He had a vein," wrote Cowell, "of strong scorn of all self-indulgence in him." When an acquaintance who had been having a glass of wine in his company left the room, FitzGerald said, with an air of great disgust, "Did you notice how he took up his glass? I am sure he likes it. Bah!"

At the same time he was full, in certain moods, of geniality and kindness. He loved to provide expensive and even elaborate entertainments for his fisherman friends. He was whimsically generous with his money; he would advance loans in cases which he thought to be deserving, and refuse to be repaid. At the same time he was not popular in the neighbourhood; he was thought highly eccentric, and the words "dotty" and "soft" were freely applied to him by the country-people. He was aware of this himself, and often consoled himself by saying frankly that all FitzGeralds were mad.

The truth is, that though a man of great intellectual power, much nobleness and tenderness of character, he was not cast quite enough in the ordinary mould for his own convenience. He just did not possess the ordinary hold on the conventional methods and usages of life which is accepted as the test of the capacity for simple citizenship. Many people are fond of their own habits and their own ways. But when this tendency is pursued so far that a man constantly deviates in small points from the habits of ordinary people, he is bound to acquire a reputation for eccentricity which vitiates his influence and causes him to be regarded with a certain compassionate contempt. We who have the opportunity of looking deeper may resolutely disregard this in the light of his high achievements and his great friendships. But the fact remains that this uncertainty, this fitfulness, this helplessness, as he himself called it, was a sign of weakness rather than of strength.

FitzGerald rather drifted into than deliberately adopted his loosely strung mode of life. He constantly deplored the absence of practical activities in his own existence, and pressed the advisability of action on his friends. "She wishes to exert herself," he wrote of his sister, Mrs. de Soyres, "which is the highest wish a FitzGerald can form." No doubt he also wished to exert himself; but his attitude may remind us of the story told by the naturalist Buckland, of the monkey that crept into the big kettle that had just been set on the fire, finding the water agreeably warm; and then, as the temperature increased, made some attempts to extricate himself, but found the contrast of the outer air each time so distressing, that he had not the courage to face it; and ended by being nearly boiled alive.

I suppose that FitzGerald did not realise, until it was too late, that practical life was becoming more impossible to him every year; he stood, as it were, shivering on the brink, half hoping that something might determine a step which he had not the courage spontaneously to take. At last he resigned himself to his fate, and devoted himself to warding off as far as possible the shadow of ennui, and the assaults of melancholy.

And a melancholy life it was. "His life," said one of his friends, "is a succession of sighs, each stifled ere half uttered; for the uselessness of sighing is as evident to him as the reason of it."

But in this we cannot acquit him of a certain lack of moral courage. We may justify a man who, recognising in himself certain powers and aptitudes, deliberately adopts a mode of life, however unconventional, in which such powers have free play. But FitzGerald's choice was not a deliberate one. He put

M

off the decision from month to month, and from year
to year, till there was nothing left to decide.   Again,
there is a still further lack of self-respect to be condemned in his shabby, desultory, slovenly habits of life.
A hermit who is deliberately dirty and uncomfortable,
because he attaches a certain moral weight to the
avoidance of all the conveniences and conventionalities
of life, may be admired at a distance, though his admirers may shun personal contact.   He is at all events
the victim of a theory.   But there is not so much to be
said for a man like FitzGerald, who had the instincts
of a gentleman, and a knowledge of the usages of the
world.   It may be tiresome to be shaved and brushed
and decently habited; but the man who cannot sustain
the trouble involved in arriving at this result is a
social malingerer.   Austerity is one thing and slovenliness is another.   The most that can be said for
FitzGerald is that his sloppiness was innocent.   But
it was not only a superficial sloppiness; it penetrated
the mind and character as well; and though no
criticisms can derogate from the abundant charm, the
delicate tenderness, the refinement, the sweetness, the
fancy, the humour of the man, yet it is impossible in
reading his letters to resist the wish that he would, so
to speak, pull himself together.   One feels that the fine
qualities of his mind and character would have gained
rather than have suffered by a little more discipline,
a little more self-control.

The possibilities of such a life as he led were great.
FitzGerald enjoyed absolute liberty, and never felt
the pressure of pecuniary anxieties.   But by his want
of method, his whimsical pettishness, his lack of
initiative and diligence, his slovenliness, he somehow
failed to make his life a wholly dignified one.

No one ever wrote with more insight than Fitz-

Gerald of the delights and pains of the idle life.   And
this is what perhaps saddens one most—that he saw
his own case with absolute lucidity, and was under no
delusions in the matter.   He deprecated any attempt
to confer upon him a dignity to which he laid no claim.
He wrote to F. Tennyson :—

"It really gives me pain to hear you or any one else call
me a philosopher, or any good thing of the sort.   I am none,
never was ; and, if I pretended to be so, was a hypocrite.
Some things, as wealth, rank, respectability, I don't care a
straw about ; but no one can resent the toothache more, nor
fifty other little ills beside that flesh is heir to.   But let us
leave all this."

At first, perhaps, he was inclined to take up a more
philosophical standpoint ; to think of himself as a
shadow-haunted dreamer.   It is true that his life
seemed very purposeless ; and yet the purposes to
which he saw others devote their lives seemed to him
more dreary and unsubstantial still, and not more
innocent.   He wrote, in 1839, to Bernard Barton, after
giving a description of his occupations :—

". . . For all which idle ease I think I must be damned.
I begin to have dreadful suspicions that this fruitless way of
life is not looked upon with satisfaction by the open eyes
above.   One really ought to dip for a little misery : perhaps
however all this ease is only intended to turn sour by-and-
bye, and so to poison one by the very nature of self-indulgence.
Perhaps, again, as idleness is so very great a trial of virtue,
the idle man who keeps himself tolerably chaste, etc., may
deserve the highest reward : the more idle, the more deserving.   Really I don't jest : but I don't propound these things
as certain."

Yet there was no one who, from sad and listless
experience, could speak so forcibly and directly of the
need of activity, the stimulus of practical life.   Thus
he wrote to Mrs. Browne :—

" *I* can vouch with all the rest whom I have known like myself, that there is no happiness but with some settled plan of *action* before one."

And again to W. F. Pollock :—

"I have been all my life apprentice to this heavy business of idleness ; and am not yet master of my craft ; the Gods are too just to suffer that I should."

And again, with the thought in his mind that so much of the activity he saw about him was mere vanity and vexation of spirit :—

"I believe I love poetry almost as much as ever : but then I have been suffered to doze all these years in the enjoyment of old childish habits and sympathies, without being called on to more active and serious duties of life. I have not put away childish things, though a man. But, at the same time, this visionary inactivity is better than the mischievous activity of so many I see about me ; not better than the useful and virtuous activity of a few others : John Allen among the number."

And in the same strain :—

"They say it is a very bad Thing to do Nothing : but I am sure that is not the case with those who are born to Blunder ; I always find that I have to repent of what I have done, not what I have left undone ; and poor W. Browne used to say it was better even to repent of what [was] undone than done."

But he could urge the activity he could not practise upon others. He wrote to W. H. Thompson :—

"I dare say you are right about an Apprenticeship in Red Tape being necessary to make a Man of Business : but is it too late in Life for you to buckle to and screw yourself up to condense some of your Lectures and scholarly Lore into a Book ? By 'too late in Life' I mean too late to take Heart to do it."

Then when he tried to rouse himself, and took

a taste of London bustle, his heart drew him back
to the country.   He wrote to Bernard Barton in
1842 :—

> "In this big London, all full of intellect and pleasure and
> business, I feel pleasure in dipping down into the country, and
> rubbing my hand over the cool dew upon the pastures, as it
> were.   I know very few people here : and care for fewer ;
> I believe I should like to live in a small house just outside
> a pleasant English town all the days of my life, making myself
> useful in a humble way, reading my books, and playing a
> rubber of whist at night.   But England cannot expect long
> such a reign of inward quiet as to suffer men to dwell so
> easily to themselves.   But Time will tell us :
>> " 'Come what come may,   .
>> Time and the Hour runs through the roughest day.' "

And when he was content, he managed to get rid
of misgivings.   He wrote to Mrs. Charlesworth in
1844 :—

> "I get radishes to eat for breakfast of a morning : with
> them comes a savour of earth that brings all the delicious
> gardens of the world back into one's soul, and almost draws
> tears from one's eyes."

Or again, to Frederic Tennyson, in a still more
exalted mood :—

> "I remember you did not desire to hear about my garden,
> which is now gorgeous with large red poppies, and lilac irises
> —satisfactory colouring : and the trees murmur a continuous
> soft *chorus to the solo which my soul discourses within.*"

But then the dreary round of life would settle down
upon him.   He wrote to W. F. Pollock :—

> "Oh, if you were to hear 'Where and oh where is my
> Soldier Laddie gone' played every three hours in a languid
> way by the Chimes of Woodbridge Church, wouldn't you
> wish to hang yourself?   On Sundays we have the 'Sicilian
> Mariner's Hymn'—very slow indeed.   I see, however, by a
> Handbill in the Grocer's Shop that a Man is going to lecture

on the Gorilla in a few weeks.   So there is something to look
forward to."

The thought which paralysed FitzGerald, with the
strong instinct for perfection which he had, was that
his own equipment was so slight and one-sided.   He
wanted time, time to study and amass knowledge, and
then time to arrange it.   He wrote to Allen :—

"I don't know any one who has thought out anything so
little as I have. I don't see to any end, and should keep silent
till I have got a little more, and that little better arranged."

But life seemed so short, and the perplexity so great,
that he found himself reduced to despair at the thought
of all the lines of thought that had to be mastered, the
systems that had to be harmonised.

He wrote to Cowell in one of these moods :—

". . . A book is to me what Locke says that watching the
hour hand of a clock is to all ; other thoughts (and those of
the idlest and seemingly most irrelevant) will intrude between
my vision and the written words : and then I have to read
over again ; often again and again, till all is crossed and
muddled. If Life were to be very much longer than is the
usual lot of men, one would try very hard to reform this
lax habit, and clear away such a system of gossamer associa-
tion : even as it is, I try to turn all wandering fancy out of
doors, and listen attentively to Whately's Logic, and old
Spinoza still ! "

Sometimes he dropped into a mood of pettish
pessimism ; and nothing better illustrates his aloof-
ness from life than that his dislike of the new mannerisms of talk and society, which he began to
encounter, should have seemed to him not matters of
indifference, but food for the profoundest melancholy.
That is the inevitable penalty which fastidious men
who stand apart from the rapid current of life have
to pay.

Yet he could sometimes rise into a higher and more hopeful vein, but too rarely.   He wrote to F. Tennyson :—

"In the meantime, all goes on toward better and better, as is my firm belief : and humanity grows clear by flowing, (very little profited by any single sage or hero) and man shall have wings to fly and something much better than that in the end. . . ."

Of practical politics FitzGerald took but little heed. Tennyson once said with much perspicacity that patriotism was not nearly so common a virtue as was supposed; but it is probably equally true, from a different point of view, that it is far more common than one would imagine.   Love of liberty and love of country are so much taken for granted by Englishmen that it does not occur to them to indulge in protestations on the subject.   Just as a normal man is not conscious of health until he begins to lose it, so the silence of Englishmen on these points may be taken as a sign that neither the freedom of the individual nor the independence of England has been of late years seriously endangered.   FitzGerald did not concern himself with the details of politics.   "Don't write politics," he wrote to F. Tennyson in 1853 ; "I agree with you beforehand."   But still he had a very deep and true devotion to his country, which only occasionally came to the surface ; as he wrote to Thompson :—

"I like that such men as Frederic [Tennyson] should be abroad : so strong, haughty, and passionate. They keep up the English character abroad. . . ."

In a half-generous, half-pessimistic mood, he wrote to Frederic Tennyson :—

"Well, say as you will, there is not, and never was, such a

country as Old England, never were there such a Gentry as the English.   They will be the distinguishing mark and glory of England in History, as the Arts were of Greece, and War of Rome.   I am sure no travel would carry me to any land so beautiful as the good sense, justice, and liberality of my good countrymen make this.   And I cling closer to it, because I feel that we are going down the hill, and shall perhaps live ourselves to talk of all this independence as a thing that has been.   To none of which you assent perhaps. At all events, my paper is done, and it is time to have done with this solemn letter.   I can see you sitting at a window that looks out on the bay of Naples, and Vesuvius with a faint smoke in the distance : a half-naked man under you cutting up water-melons, etc.   Haven't I seen it all in Annuals, and in the Ballet of *Masaniello* long ago ?"

As the years went on, the hopefulness decreased, the pessimism grew upon him; but it is clear that he only took a poetical view of politics.   He loved the spirit of a land that was so free and so beautiful, but he cared little for the history of the steps by which her fair pre-eminence had been won; he would have agreed with Clough that for a Greek the important thing was that the battle of Marathon should have been fought; but that to know how and when it had been fought mattered little.

Occasionally he plunged boldly into large philosophical speculations.   The opening panorama which science appeared likely to reveal to men he treats of in a lofty vein in a letter to Cowell :—

"Yet, as I often think, it is not the poetical imagination, but bare Science that every day more and more unrolls a greater Epic than the *Iliad*; the History of the World, the infinitudes of Space and Time !   I never take up a book of Geology or Astronomy but this strikes me.   And when we think that Man must go on to discover in the same plodding way, one fancies that the Poet of to-day may as well fold his

hands, or turn them to dig and delve, considering how soon
the march of discovery will distance all his imaginations, [and]
dissolve the language in which they are uttered. Martial, as
you say, lives now, after two thousand years ; a space that
seems long to us whose lives are so brief ; but a moment, the
twinkling of an eye, if compared (not to Eternity alone) but
to the ages which it is now known the world must have
existed, and (unless for some external violence) must continue
to exist. Lyell, in his book about America, says that the falls
of Niagara, if (as seems certain) they have worked their way
back southwards for seven miles, must have taken over
35,000 years to do so, at the rate of something over a foot a
year ! Sometimes they fall back on a stratum that crumbles
away from behind them more easily : but then again they
have to roll over rock that yields to them scarcely more per-
ceptibly than the anvil to the serpent. And those very soft
strata which the Cataract now erodes contain evidences of a
race of animals, and of the action of seas washing over them,
long before Niagara came to have a distinct current ; and the
rocks were compounded ages and ages before those strata !
So that, as Lyell says, the Geologist looking at Niagara forgets
even the roar of its waters in the contemplation of the awful
processes of time that it suggests. It is not only that this
vision of Time must wither the Poet's hope of immortality ;
but it is in itself more wonderful than all the conceptions of
Dante and Milton."

What he felt about religion and religious specula-
tion is not difficult to divine. He was deeply stirred,
it is clear, in early days by the strong, vital faith of
Matthews the evangelist; but the bent of his whole
mind was towards scepticism. He was heard once in
his later life murmuring to himself the words, " Though
your sins be as scarlet, they shall be as white as snow;
though they be red like crimson, they shall be as
wool "; but the utterance is to be attributed, I believe,
more to a sense of the haunting beauty of the words
than to any religious motive. The most precise and

definite religious systems, after all, can only profess to
touch the fringe of the deep and perennial mysteries
of life.   They serve to brighten only the crescent
edge of the shadowy orb, and leave the dark tracts
unrevealed.   The mystery of pain, of evil, of the
future life, of the brevity of existence—these cannot be solved.   The utmost that religion can do is to
illuminate a few yards of the glimmering pathway,
and say that the descending darkling stair must be
trodden in the light of Faith.   But a mind like Fitz-
Gerald's demanded more certainty.   Though he saw
clearly that he himself and minds like his own, acute,
questioning, unsatisfied minds, must be condemned to
doubt, he held strong and sensible views on the
benefits of religion for the community, for simpler
minds and hearts.   He wrote a very remarkable letter
to Carlyle on the subject :—

"I was very glad of your letter : especially as regards that
part in it about the Derbyshire villages. In many other parts
of England (not to mention my own Suffolk) you would find
the same substantial goodness among the people, resulting (as
you say) from the funded virtues of many good humble men
gone by. I hope you will continue to teach us all, as you
have done, to make some use and profit of all this : at least, not
to let what good remains to die away under penury and neglect.
I also hope you will have some mercy now, and in future, on
the 'Hebrew rags' which are grown offensive to you ; considering that it was these rags that really did bind together
those virtues which have transmitted down to us all the good
you noticed in Derbyshire. If the old creed was so com-
mendably effective in the Generals and Counsellors of two
hundred years ago, I think we may be well content to let it
work still among the ploughmen and weavers of to-day ; and
even to suffer some absurdities in the Form, if the Spirit does
well upon the whole. Even poor Exeter Hall ought, I think,
to be borne with ; it is at least better than the wretched

Oxford business. When I was in Dorsetshire some weeks ago, and saw chancels done up in Sky-blue and gold, with niches, candles, an *Altar*, rails to keep off the profane laity, and the parson (like your Reverend Mr. Hitch [1]) *intoning* with his back to the people, I thought the Exeter Hall war-cry of ' The Bible—the whole Bible—and nothing but the Bible ' a good cry : I wanted Oliver and his Dragoons to march in and put an end to it all. Yet our Established Parsons (when quiet and in their senses) make good country gentlemen, and magistrates ; and I am glad to secure one man of means and education in each parish of England : the people can always resort to Wesley, Bunyan, and Baxter, if they want stronger food than the old Liturgy, and the orthodox Discourse. I think you will not read what I have written : or be very bored with it. But it *is* written now."

Meanwhile he lived as best he might. In such current conceptions of religion he could not rest. He could but say with a wistful affectation of cynicism :—

" Qu'est-ce que cela fait si je m'amuse ?"

And in the presence of hopeless failure and grief— " I do not know ; I cannot help : and I distress myself as little as I can."

And then, with a gentle tolerance for a life which seemed, as he looked back upon it, both ineffective and full of mistakes :—

" . . . I wait here, partly because of Nieces and Nephews on either hand of me, and partly to give time for a little Flower and Leaf to come up inland. Also, a little absurd Lodging is so much pleasanter than the grave House one built. What Blunders one has to look back on, to be sure ! So many, luckily, that one has ceased to care for any *one*. Walpole congratulated himself on one point : knowing what he wanted : I fancy you are wise in that also. But for most of us—

    " ' Man is but Man, and what he most desires,
       Pleases at first : then pleases not ; then tires ! ' "

---

[1] *v.* Carlyle's *Cromwell*, vol. i. p. 193 (1st ed.).

It is, after all, a melancholy picture. Not without
loss can a man withdraw himself from the world and
shirk the primal inheritance of labour. Our admiration
of the man and of his best work cannot blind us to the
fact that this irresolution, this languid lingering upon
the skirts of life, is not a beautiful nor an admirable
thing. If the sacrifice had been made in the interests
of art, it would have been different; but FitzGerald
had no illusions on this point either. He often insists
on the cardinal truth that life is above art, that art is
a service, not a dominion: that art must minister to
life, not life to art. There is a certain priestly mood
which falls upon those in whom the need for creating
what is beautiful is very imperious. FitzGerald had
none of this; he would have laughed at it as a species
of pretentiousness. In this he was not necessarily right,
but we are endeavouring to present his view of the
case. The solemnity of Wordsworth, the affectation
of Tennyson, were not only mistaken in FitzGerald's
view, but slightly grotesque; and thus we have the
pathetic spectacle of a man choosing to hold aloof from
life in a way that could only have been justified if it
had been the result of a deliberate theory, a constrain-
ing vocation. We see him regretting his own indecision,
and urging on his friends the imperative duty of
taking a hand in the game; and yet unable to put
his theories into practice, and trifling with life in a
melancholy rather than in a cynical spirit. FitzGerald
is thus, as I have said, a Hamlet of literature, clear-
sighted, full of the sense of mystery and wonder and
beauty; yet unable to dedicate himself to the creative
life, from lack of a certain vitality, and from an unhappy capacity of seeing both sides of a question; and
yet from indolence and irresolution unable to throw
in his lot with the humdrum cares and duties that,

after all, bring peace and content into the majority of lives.

Yet these are but the shadows of temperament; deep in FitzGerald's heart lay an abundance of simple treasures. He was loving and loyal; quietly and unostentatiously generous; indolent as he was, he would take endless trouble in details to serve his friends. He was pure-minded with an almost virginal delicacy. "FitzGerald and Spedding," said W. H. Thompson, "were two of the purest-living men among my intimates." But besides the effusiveness of sentiment which weakened FitzGerald for practical life, there was another tendency likely to beset a sensitive nature. He lived little in the future, and much in the past. The thought that a happy day was passing clouded his enjoyment of it; the remembrance of the days that are no more came in like a shadow between him and the present. This he endeavoured to meet by cultivating as far as he could a stoical attitude. He tried, like Goethe, with the sensitive instinct for sparing himself pain, not to grieve; feeling that if he dwelt upon the thought of death or loss, it would break his burdened heart. Thus, even in the midst of a tender and delicate retrospect, we are checked as it were by a sudden chill. It was probably this reluctance to suffer, this emotional indolence, that deprived FitzGerald of that supreme gift of poetry. It is hard to say how the greatest and most sensitive of poets bear their grief; perhaps the secret is that, together with the intensity of suffering, they have a similarly strong power of recuperation. They descend inevitably into the dark; and when they have emerged again they can say what they have seen. But even this luxury of literary emotion was denied to FitzGerald, because he could

not face the suffering that is a necessary condition of
the song.   Once in his life he went deep and bore the
spoils away; in Omar he faced the darkest thoughts
that lay at the bottom of his heart, and spoke out.

But otherwise his literary occupations were planned
more to deaden than to quicken thought.   He took
refuge in translations and selections.   He was too
restless to be wholly inactive.   Yet the sight of perfection, of great thoughts nobly expressed, did not quicken
him to emulation, but rather encouraged him to stand
aside and to take refuge in judging; in knowing by
trained instinct and practical appreciation how far
perfection had been attained.

I imagine that FitzGerald's one haunting thought
was regret.   An impersonal regret for all the beauty
and charm of the world that flowered only to die; and
a more personal regret that he had not been able to
put out his powers to do and to be.   He was overshadowed by a constant sense of the brevity, the
fleeting swiftness of time, the steady, irrevocable
lapsing of life to death.   Melancholy takes many
forms; in some it finds its materials in anxious and
gloomy forebodings of what the future may bring or
take away; with some the present seems irremediably
dreary.   But FitzGerald lived in a wistful regret for
the beautiful hours that were gone, the days that are
no more.   Tennyson called this feeling "the passion
of the past," but said that in his own case it was not a
sadness born of experience, but rather the luxurious
melancholy of youth; and that with him it tended to
diminish as the years went on.   But with FitzGerald
it was, it seems, an ever-present sense.   Beneath and
behind the sweet sounds and sights of the earth that he
loved so well, he heard the sullen echo of a voice that
warned him that all was passing away.   "It gives me,"

he wrote, "a strange sort of Pleasure to walk about
the old Places among the falling leaves once more."
As the golden light of evening crept over the pastures,
touching tree and field with the strange and sweet
tranquillity of bright outline and lengthened shadow,
he said within his heart that it was all exquisitely and
profoundly beautiful, but that the sweet hour was
numbered with the past even as he gazed. All present
enjoyment was darkened for FitzGerald by the pressure
of this insistent thought. As the sweet summer day
rose, shone, waned, he wrote to Cowell in India :—

"I am sitting as of old in my accustomed Bedroom, looking
out on a Landscape which your Eyes would drink. It is said
there has not been such a Flush of Verdure for years : and
they are making hay on the Lawn before the house, so as one
wakes to the tune of the Mower's Scythe-whetting, and with
the old Perfume blowing in at open windows. . . .

"June over ! A thing I think of with Omar-like sorrow.
And the Roses here are blowing—and going—as abundantly
as even in Persia. I am still at Geldestone, and still looking
at Omar by an open window which gives over a Greener
Landscape than yours."

And in the sad days of his married life, dreaming of
the old congenial friendships, he wrote to Cowell :—

"Shall we ever meet again ? I think not ; or not in such
plight, both of us, as will make Meeting what it used to be.
Only to-day I have been opening dear old Salámán : the
original Copy we bought and began this time three years ago
at Oxford ; with all my scratches of Query and Explanation
in it, and the Notes from you among the Leaves. How often I
think with Sorrow of my many Harshnesses and Impatiences !
which are yet more of manner than Intention. My wife is sick
of hearing me sing in a doleful voice the old Glee of ' When shall
we Three Meet again ?' Especially the Stanza, 'Though in
foreign Lands we sigh, Parcht beneath a hostile Sky,' etc.
How often too I think of the grand Song written by some
Scotch Lady, which I sing to myself for you on Ganges Banks !"

With this personal sense of loss went a deeper sense
of the endless pathos of the world, of the sadness
which is yet in itself beautiful. The following frag-
ment is like a vignette of Bewick; the crumbling
walls, the singing bird, and the old man feeling that
his own feeble life was lapsing into ruin too :—

"I have at last bid adieu to poor old Dunwich : the Robin
singing in the Ivy that hangs on those old Priory walls. A
month ago I wrote to ask Carlyle's Niece about her Uncle,
and telling her of this Priory, and how her Uncle would once
have called me Dilettante ; all which she read to him ; he
only said 'Poor, Poor old Priory !'"

He was ever sensitive to these slight, wistful, fugitive
effects : here is a little bit of sweet humanity—
wholesome and tender like the man's own loving
heart :—

"When I was in Paris in 1830, just before that Revolution,
I stopped one Evening on the Boulevards by the Madeleine to
listen to a Man who was singing to his Barrel-organ. Several
passing 'Blouses' had stopped also : not only to listen, but to
join in the Songs, having bought little *Libretti* of the words
from the Musician. I bought one too ; for, I suppose, the
smallest French Coin ; and assisted in the Song which the
Man called out beforehand (as they do Hymns at Church),
and of which I enclose you the poor little Copy. ' *Le Bon
Pasteur*, s'il vous plaît'—I suppose the Circumstances : the
'beau temps,' the pleasant Boulevards, the then so amiable
People, all contributed to the effect this Song had upon me ;
anyhow, it has constantly revisited my memory for these forty-
three years ; and I was thinking, the other day, touched me
more than any of Béranger's most beautiful Things. This,
however, may be only one of 'Old Fitz's' Crotchets, as
Tennyson and others would call them."

And again in the letter which relates to the death
of George Crabbe of Bredfield, which gives a fine
instance of his sober grief, neither forced nor self-

conscious, he puts into words that dreary sense of
sadness which all know, which is aroused by the sight
of all the little arrangements and furniture of a life,
the trifling objects of daily, familiar use, when that life
slips suddenly into the darkness :—

"You may imagine it was melancholy enough to me to
revisit the old house when He who had made it so warm for
me so often lay cold in his Coffin unable to entertain me
any more ! His little old dark Study (which I called the
Cobblery) smelt strong of its old Smoke : and the last
Cheroot he had tried lay three-quarters smoked in its little
China ash-pan. This I have taken as a Relic, as also a little
silver Nutmeg Grater which used to give the finishing Touch to
many a Glass of good hot Stuff, and also had belonged to the
Poet Crabbe. . . ."

And in FitzGerald's heart, behind the sorrow of the
world, lay the strong yearning to be loved, to be
remembered, to leave something which, when the book
of life is shut, should still mingle with the current of
the world's life and hold its place there.

". . . It is a very odd thing, but quite true, I assure you,
that before your letter came I was sitting at breakfast alone,
and reading some of Moore's Songs, and thinking to myself
how it was fame enough to have written but one song—air,
or words—which should in after days solace the sailor at the
wheel, or the soldier in foreign places !—be taken up into the
life of England ! No doubt 'The Last Rose of Summer' will
accomplish this."

It may be said that all this belongs to the region of
luxurious and self-conscious emotion ; and that the
sorrows and activities of life leave but little room for
dalliance with such frail and wistful thoughts. But if
so, then the pressure of real life is a hardening and a
coarsening thing ; and further, there must be many,
even among those who are moving among realities, for

N

whom in quiet hours such thoughts must lie in wait. We may label them unmanly and unreal; but it is an unjust and tyrannical mood that would thus deal with the twilight thoughts of the heart.   Between the sunshine and the dark there are infinite gradations, and it is in the perception of these softer and more delicate emotions, these thoughts that arise and are born between the darkness and the day, that the incommunicable essence of wonder and delight consists.   And whether we approve or no, it was in this half-lit region that FitzGerald's life was spent.   Some would perhaps say that his ethical and religious views were the cause of his half-heartedness.   Thompson, the Master of Trinity, uttered the shallow dictum that FitzGerald was a prisoner in Doubting Castle, as though by an effort he might have escaped and fared forward.   But FitzGerald's vague religious views were the effect of temperament, and not the cause of his failure.   He was not one who could take a creed on trust.   And even a creed is, as it were, only a surface solution, and gives no explanation of the dark mystery of life and death, and heeds it not except in so far as it can trample over it in courageous disregard.   "Healing is well," FitzGerald might have said, "but wherefore wounds to heal?"   A creed is a refuge of ardent and practical natures, who feel that they must put in for the struggle and try to amend what God somehow seems to allow to be amiss.   But one who has no power of practical activity sinks deeper and deeper into the darkness of the question why so much must be amiss, and what all this weary strife denotes.

It is hard to say whether enforced activity would have saved FitzGerald, but it is certain that, given the conditions of his life, the shadow was inevitable.   As FitzGerald sadly wrote in his version of *The Mighty*

Magician, in lines where it is hard to believe he had not himself in mind :—

> " Well, each his way and humour ; some to lie
> Like Nature's sickly children in her lap,
> While all the stronger brethren are at play."

FitzGerald possessed, in a strong degree, a spectacular habit of mind. His failure in the region of practical activities was due mainly to the fact that he stood aloof from life, and watched it, sometimes with a mournful wonder, sometimes with a humorous jest, stream past him, the pictures taking shape and becoming blurred, the groups gathering and dissolving, as in a fantastic dream.

Thus he writes to Allen :—

". . . My brother John's wife, always delicate, has had an attack this year, which she can never get over : and while we are all living in this house cheerfully, she lives in separate rooms, can scarcely speak to us, or see us : and bears upon her cheek the marks of death. She has shown great Christian dignity all through her sickness : was the only cheerful person when they supposed she could not live : and is now very composed and happy. You say sometimes how like things are to dreams . or, as I think, to the shifting scenes of a play. So does this place seem to me. All our family, except my mother, are collected here : all my brothers and sisters, with their wives, husbands, and children : sitting at different occupations, or wandering about the grounds and gardens, discoursing each their separate concerns, but all united into one whole. The weather is delightful : and when I see them passing to and fro, and hear their voices, it is like scenes of a play. I came here only yesterday."

He had no desire to step down and mingle with the flowing tide ; still less to modify or direct the action of the play ; so he loitered apart in his green garden, noting, approving, wondering, moralising, not a man, but the shadow of a man.

The instinct which lay deepest of all in FitzGerald's
nature was the need of affection. In early days this
was so urgent, that he had even no difficulty in giving
it voice. He wrote to Allen, welcoming a letter from
the latter :—

"It has indeed been a long time coming ; but it is all the
more delicious. Perhaps you can't imagine how wistfully I
have looked for it : how, after a walk, my eyes have turned
to the table, on coming into the room, to see it. Sometimes
I have been tempted to be angry with you : but then I
thought that I was sure that you would come a hundred miles
to serve me, though you were too lazy to sit down to a letter.
I suppose that people who are engaged in serious ways of life,
and are of well-filled minds, don't think much about the
interchange of letters with any anxiety : but I am an idle
fellow, of a very ladylike turn of sentiment : and my friendships are more like loves, I think."

All through his life we see him constrained into
friendships, not the quiet, unromantic friendships of an
ordinary man, but strong, almost unbalanced preoccupations. But even these became, as time went on,
more and more difficult to maintain, owing to Fitz-
Gerald's invincible shyness in the presence even of
those whom he loved, his dislike of change, his increasing desire for seclusion.

Even in the case of the beloved Cowell, after his
absence in India, FitzGerald had a great difficulty in
picking up the dropped threads. He wrote :—

". . . I hope you don't think I have forgotten you. Your
visit gave me a sad sort of Pleasure, dashed with the Memory
of other Days ; I now see so few People, and those all of the
common sort, with whom I never talk of our old Subjects ; so
I get in some measure unfitted for such converse, and am
almost saddened with the remembrance of an old contrast

when it comes.   And there is something besides ; a Shadow
of Death : but I won't talk of such things : only believe I
don't forget you, nor wish to be forgotten by you.   Indeed,
your kindness touched me."

And he becomes more averse to making the personal
acquaintance even of those with whom, as a correspondent, he was on almost intimate terms ; to make a
new acquaintance in person was evidently of the nature
of a terror to the diffident man.

But in spite of his own diffidence, to be surrounded
with love seemed to FitzGerald the one thing worth
having in the world.   Writing of a friend, who had
lately been left a widow, he said :—

"She, though a wretchedly sickly woman, and within two
months of her confinement when he died, has somehow
weathered it all beyond Expectation.   She has her children
to attend to, and be her comfort in turn : and though having
lost what most she loved yet has something to love still, and
to be beloved by.   There are worse Conditions than that."

And again of a devoted friendship between two
boatmen :—

"I tell Newson he has at last found his Master, and become
possessed of that troublesome thing : an anxious Regard for
some one."

One of the most salient features of FitzGerald's
whole view of life is this.   He expected so much from
it : his mind was like a sensitive plate which catches
impressions with delicate fidelity ; and the result was
that to FitzGerald every moment was an occasion.
The glance of an eye, the gesture of a hand, the ivy
on a ruined wall, the piping of a bird, the glitter of
light on the leaves of a forest tree when the sun
flares high overhead, the rolling up of great piles of

cloud, the gliding plunge of a ship under a press of
canvas—all these things came home to him with a
sharp shock of pleasure. He was a lyrical poet in his
power of taking hold of an isolated impression of
some beautiful thing, but without the power of lyrical
expression. The danger of such a temperament is
that it demands too many of these impressions, and
that life does not provide enough of them; besides,
it is not enough that they should be there; there must
be also a certain harmony of mood, a power of interpretation, a zest which it is not always in the power
of the spirit to secure. Thus FitzGerald was in a
certain high and emotional region a sensualist. A
sensualist is generally understood to be a man with
a keen appetite for strong and, as a rule, debasing
sensations. But it is possible to be a sensualist in a
higher world, the world of beauty. It is possible to
have a certain uncontrolled avidity for beauty, and to
be ill-content with the leagues of commonplace life
that must be traversed without the coincidence of
mood and beauty. Such a temperament can bring
a man many moments of pleasure, but it can hardly
bring happiness; and it is almost inevitable that as
the perceptions grow blunted and as vital energies
decrease, a shadow should settle down upon the mind.
This is to be clearly detected in FitzGerald's letters.
He was, indeed, too much of a gentleman to inflict
his moods directly upon his correspondent. His
letters were often written with a kind of delicate
courtesy, a desire to give pleasure to his reader; but
none the less is it clear that in much weariness and in
a settled sadness he was beguiling the time as best
he could, the time that denied him the joys he
desired.

FitzGerald seems to catch regretfully at the flying

moment, that strange passing current that may not be delayed ; even as he says, "Here is joy and beauty," the moment is gone. He was often face to face with the mystery that there is really no such thing as the present; the future beckons at first far off, then near ; then even in the swift passage of thought when a man says of a sweet moment, "It is here," it is numbered with the past. There may be other beautiful moments in store for the heart, but never exactly the same again. Thus all FitzGerald's moments of happiness were clouded by the thought that all was passing, moving, changing. In his case this never turns to bitterness, but it turns to a mournful patience :—

> " One Moment in Annihilation's Waste,
> One Moment, of the Well of Life to taste—
> 　The Stars are setting and the Caravan
> Starts for the Dawn of Nothing—Oh, make haste ! "

Yet it is this very mood that gives FitzGerald his sad and strange power over the mind, for these are things that all have felt and have experienced ; and what matters, after all, in a poet is not that the thing should be profitable, but that it should be true, so long as it is also made beautiful. For disguise it as we will by activities and by pleasures, we live under a shadow of doom. We may beguile it, we may banish it, but the tolling of the bell that heralds the end beats in our ears ; and we can but live soberly and innocently, taking all into account. He is wisest who can face the solemn music, and who, if he cannot be happy himself, can at least strive to contribute to the happiness of those to whom his heart goes out, who are bound upon the same mysterious pilgrimage.

The question that remains is this : To what extent is a man bound to the service of men ? The answer is

immensely complicated by the constitution of society,
especially by the social order which authorises a man
to live without labour upon the accumulations made
by his ancestors.   Given the shy and sensitive temperament, the acute and sceptical mind, the indolent
disposition of FitzGerald, and the ample competence
which he enjoyed, and the resultant was bound to be
what it was.   He was too sensitive to take his
ambitions into the arena, too indolent to submit his
kindly impulses to an organised system of philan-
thropy ; too uncertain to preach a faith which he could
not hold.   But it may be questioned whether the
primal law which seems to indicate labour as a condition of bodily and mental equilibrium can ever be
quite successfully evaded.   FitzGerald felt the need
of organised work in his own life, but the pressure
was never strong enough to induce him to submit
himself to uneasy conditions.

After all, the process of estimating the character
even of the best of men must be of the nature of
addition and subtraction.   It is the final total that
is our main concern.   In FitzGerald's case, on the
debit side of the account stand a certain childish-
ness of disposition, indolence, a weak sentimentality,
a slackness of moral fibre, a deep-seated infirmity of
purpose.   These may be partly condoned by an inherited eccentricity.   On the credit side stand a true
loyalty of nature, an unobtrusive generosity, a real love
of humanity, a moral clear-sightedness, an acute perception of beauty, a literary gift that at its best was of the
nature of genius.   There can be little question on
which side the balance lies.   We may regret the want
of strenuousness, the over-developed sensibility which
led him to live constantly in the pathos of the past,
the pain of the contemplation of perishable sweetness.

But we may be thankful for so simple, so tender-hearted, so ingenuous a life; we may feel that the long, quiet years were not misspent which produced, if so rarely, the delicate flowers of genius.   To enrich the world with one imperishable poem, to make music of some of the saddest and darkest doubts that haunt the mind of man—this is what many far busier and more concentrated lives fail to do.   To strew the threshold of the abyss with flowers, to dart an ethereal gleam into the encircling gloom, to set a garland of roses in the very shrine of death, to touch despair with beauty—this is to bear a part in the work of consoling men, of reconciling fate, of enlightening doom, of interpreting the vast and awful mind of God.   Truth itself can do no more than hint at the larger hope— "It is He that hath made us."

INDEX

Printed by T. and A. Constable, Printers to His Majesty
at the Edinburgh University Press